# The Therapist

## Other Books by Author

Copyright A Novel

Our Daughters

Diamond City A Screenplay

# The Therapist

by

Lori Lesko

ISBN-13: 978-1508994954
ISBN-10: 1508994951

# Dedication

*This novel is dedicated to anyone who struggles with Post Traumatic Stress Disorder. For more information and to seek help:*

http://www.ptsd.va.gov/

# Contents

"It's an acquired skill; in order for people to believe the truth about themselves, you have to master the art of lying."

~ Lindsey CarMichael, LCSW

# 1

## Carrie Warner

After taking one last sip of coffee, I skimmed through Carrie Warner's file. The brief notes in the folder came from the doctor who discharged her from a three-week stay in hospital.

*Carrie Warner, white female, age: twenty-three, weight: ninety pounds.*

*Admitted: December 2nd, 2013. Patient was found unresponsive on her apartment floor by her mother. Admitted by Dr. Eden, under the Baker Act, as the patient was a danger to herself due to current weight.*

*Diagnosis: Anorexia nervosa, Depression and Anxiety Disorder. She attended all group activities and individual sessions. She didn't show any interest in interacting with other patients and staff. She was caught numerous times hiding food from her plate, purely to throw it in the trash or hide it in the common area. This was the time the patient became difficult. She refused to discuss her family life and wouldn't acknowledge that she was in grave physical danger if she didn't maintain body weight.*

*Recommended: Return home on the condition of therapy, routinely checking her weight. Discharged weight: ninety-six pounds.*

*Medication: Zoloft 10 milligrams, Xanax 0.25 milligrams 2x.*

It was noted that aside from the sessions in the hospital, Carrie had never been in therapy before. I looked at the form she had been asked to fill in, and she'd written eating disorder, age twenty-three, unemployed teacher, divorced and no insurance. Not my first anorexic, but currently, she was the only one.

I brushed my hair into a bun that matched the auburn hair-clip. A few golden strands had fallen on my blouse. I applied a new round of lipstick. I stood and fluffed up the pillows on the couch and love seat. I never knew which one the patient would choose to settle upon, but it usually told me something when they did. I adjusted one of the picture frames. Placing my pen and notebook on the chair, I noticed the precise minute of the desk clock that was turned toward me: 9:00a.m.

Out in the waiting room, I forced what I hoped was a gentle and warm smile. Carrie Warner sat with her legs crossed and the top foot shaking. When she stood to greet me, I saw that her skin was almost translucent as it stretched across her cheekbones.

"Carrie Warner?" I asked, reaching out my hand.

"That's me," she replied with a skeleton smile. Her teeth seemed too large for her mouth and she was pallid, frail. She was a ghost, standing right in front of me. Her grip was weak and I felt as if her bones would break if I applied just a minuscule amount of pressure.

"I'm Lindsey CarMichael, but just call me Lindsey."

I held the door open for her and Carrie passed by me, like a waft of air. She took her time looking at all the paintings on the wall as she moved slowly into the office. She noticed the basket of toys I had left on the ground. She turned to ask permission from me.

"Where should I sit?"

"The couch or the chair, both are very comfortable," I assured her with a smile. Carrie ran her tongue over her top lip, as if this would be the biggest decision she had to make today.

"Ah... I'll take the couch," she said, looking to me in need of further approval. I obliged her with a tiny nod. Her stick figure moved at a snail's pace and parked itself at the far end of the couch, shoulders squared. She repeated her position of right leg over the left, nervously twitching the hanging foot. Seeing that she sat at the far end of the sofa, I took note of her movement, knew she was terrified and wanted no part of therapy. I needed to make her comfortable.

"Can I get you anything, some water, or tea?" I asked. *Or maybe a cheeseburger and some fries?* the sarcastic voice in my head added.

"Oh, no, no, I'm fine," she said faintly.

Lifting my pen and notepad off the chair, I sat down and exhaled. Judging by Carrie's look, this would be a tug of war Q&A session. And by my rules, in all first sessions, the patient must win. She needed to gain my trust or it ended here and now.

"So, how can I help you?" I asked cheerfully while writing some shorthand notes on Carrie's appearance.

> *Patient has long spaghetti-thin hair—talks in a whisper, wears baggy sweatshirt and jeans.*

"Did you read my hospital report?" she asked, as her mouth tightened and her eyebrows rose.

"Yes, but I like to hear what you want. How I can help you achieve your goals?" I asked with a blank face.

"I don't have any goals," she said. Her right hand rubbed her forehead and her foot moved double-time with its shaking. It appeared Carrie was too nervous to even ponder the question. I noticed a clicking sound. Studying her face, I saw Carrie was grinding her teeth. It was time to lower the pressure. Her eyes focused again on the floor and the basket of toys. It occurred to me that Carrie may have been stunted in her emotional growth. And perhaps taking her back to her childhood may be a way of getting through to her.

"Would you like to sit on the floor and see the basket?" I asked. Swiftly, her head snapped up and she gazed at me. Her hair flew into her mouth and her grassy-green eyes stretched open, almost consuming her entire face. My impression of the girl was that Carrie was all eyes, teeth and hair, nothing else. After the shock had worn off, she exhaled and answered me.

"I'm a grown woman," she said, stating the obvious.

"Yes, I am aware of your age. I just thought maybe you'd like to sit on the floor and see what's in the basket. I'll join you if you like, come on," I said, and tossed my notepad and pen on the desk. "Take off your shoes and get comfortable." I encouraged her by kicking off my own shoes first. This made Carrie genuinely smile for the first time and I saw the five-year-old in her come out.

"Okay!" she said, giggling while covering her mouth with her hand. *A sign she was not allowed to be happy.* Taking off my vest and adjusting my grey pants, I scooted down on the floor. Carrie followed me gingerly. It appeared everything she did needed approval of some sort before she could function. Together we gazed at the basket. There were Barbie dolls and stuffed animals, a few puzzles and games. Carrie innocuously reached out and picked out the stuffed teddy bear.

"Oh, that's my favorite one," I said, to see what reaction I would get.

"I'm sorry, I'm so sorry. You can have it back," she cried, offering it to me.

"No." I shook my head. "You chose him first, so he is yours."

"Are you sure?" Carrie asked with pleading eyes.

"Yep, I think I prefer the bunny rabbit anyway," I said with a smile, and picked up the pink stuffed animal.

"So you like bears, huh?"

"Yes," Carrie said, cuddling her bear. "I use to have one when I was little, his name was James." Her eyes were transfixed on the object. I decided hypnosis would work well on her.

"How old were you then?"

"I don't know." Carrie blinked a few times and suddenly became aware of her behavior. She lingered there for a second and then placed the bear back in the basket. She rushed back to her position on the sofa. "This is stupid. Please don't make me do this anymore."

"Why not?" I inquired, still sitting on the floor.

"I can't go home and tell my mother I played with toys during my therapy session. She already thinks I'm nuts to begin with."

"Oh, well, what would you like to do?" Getting up, I straightened out my pants and blouse. Then I waited for Carrie to give me the next clue.

"I guess we could talk about why I am here to begin with," she started. I made no sound and returned to my chair, picking up the pen and notepad.

"Why are you here?"

"Because I was found passed out in my apartment by my mother," she said, exhaling, her eyes glued to the floor.

"Not to mention, you're five foot ten inches and you weigh ninety pounds," I added.

Carrie appeared to be shaken not from what I had said, but because of *how* I'd said it. *Good.* "So, why do you want to die?" I asked.

She shook her head and there was a disturbing look in her eyes telling me to back off. Not yet.

While Carrie stayed frozen in her seat, I jumped up and went to the bathroom door and opened it; revealing a set of scales on the floor. Carrie watched my every move with a look of horror on her face. She shook her head back and forth—her limbs went stiff.

"Well?" I said. "If you don't believe me, let's see how much you weigh."

Carrie didn't budge. She hugged her arms around herself, and her eyes darted toward the abandoned teddy bear. She was regressing right before my eyes to that little girl again. "Carrie Warner, you're a twenty-three-year old divorced woman. Stand up and come over here and allow yourself to see what you weigh."

"I don't...don't wanna..." she breathed out.

"You don't want *to*; do not talk like a child in front of me. And yes, you will weigh yourself right now," I repeated.

Carrie snapped out of her indolent behavior. Still looking terrified, Carrie seemed unable to resist the direct command and she glided over to me like a ghost. Carrie eyed the scales then kicked off her sandals. I showed no emotion as she stood on it—calibrating the black button on the beam to a hundred pounds. All the while, she avoided looking at herself in the mirror. I made a mental note of this. Carrie shifted her weight a little and the black beam moved to the left. Carrie breathed out a gentle sigh of relief. She was content to be less than a hundred pounds.

"That makes you happy?" I inquired without sentiment.

"Yes, I mean, I'm sorry," she said.

I calibrated the scale to measure fifty pounds. It moved to the right. Carrie became anxious. She held her breath. I slowly moved the higher button across until it reached ninety-nine pounds. Carrie jumped off the scale and began sobbing.

"I've gained three pounds!" she yelled petulantly.

"And this upsets you why?" I asked.

"Don't you understand? I gained three whole pounds? It must have been from all that ridiculous hospital food they forced me to eat."

"I see," I said, lowering my eyes as I walked back to the office chair.

Carrie followed me back into the office, and seemed to think I must be angry with her, because she threw herself on the couch and began to cry.

"It must be so exhausting to be you," I said, trying to bait her.

Carrie's crying became muted as she tilted her head in my direction. She rolled her body on its side and studied me. Carrie looked like a thin piece of plywood floating on the couch. She quirked an eyebrow as we gazed at each other. She wanted to see me. Her jaw clenched. She was angry. *Good*, I thought. I needed her to wallow in her pool of rage for a little while to get the feel of it. Then she would identify the source and we could begin with our work.

"What do you mean by that?" she asked.

"Simply, that you must be exhausted. You hold everything in so deeply that the very thought of gaining a few pounds brings you to tears," I told her, resting my elbow on the side of my chair, tossing the pen on the desk. I provided her with a solemn expression. "Hell, I'm tired just looking at you," I said.

"Huh?" she cried.

"You have to know that, right?"

"You mean I have to know that I'm exhausted?"

"Yes, your body is starving for nourishment, which you deny it on a daily basis. And God knows what other little secrets you're hiding in that mesh of a brain. I say mesh because once you stop eating, your brain cells start dying. So we don't have much time to save you, unless you begin to deal with your anger."

"You're the one making me angry!" Carrie said, sitting upright.

"Really?" I asked. "I don't think that's true."

"Yes," she said.

"So, the fact that you lost your job as a teacher, or your husband divorced you, doesn't upset you? Make you angry?"

"Well, yes, it did. It does!"

"What about Mommy being too controlling of your life and not providing you with enough emotional support when you were a little girl?" I said, digging in.

Carrie pulled herself over to the far end of the couch, grabbed a pillow and squeezed it until her fingertips turned bloody red. She turned her head away from me, but I could hear her sniffles.

"Is that it?" I leaned back up against my chair. I didn't want her to feel as if I was invading her space. Carrie sobbed some more. I allowed this to continue without a word. When Carrie gained more control of herself, I stood and offered her some tissues.

She reached out and took them without a word.

"Can you tell me what happened?" I asked, sitting back down in my chair. I knew I shouldn't have given her a question she could answer with a yes or no answer, but it was our first session together. And she didn't look ready to go much deeper than she already had.

"No," she said, shaking her head.

"That's okay. Carrie, look at me."

She obeyed like a trained animal at the zoo. Her eyes were puffy and bulging out even more from her tears—making her face shrink. She veritably looked like an alien, not a twenty-three-year-old woman.

"We have to meet three times a week. Is 9:00 a.m. a good time for you?"

"Yes."

"And I want you to keep a diary of everything you eat and how you feel when you eat something, okay?"

"Does that include today? Cause all I ate were a couple of grapes," she said.

"How many?" I asked.

"Ten, but I sort of sucked on the last five."

"I know this will be hard, but you have to follow what your doctor said for your meals. Otherwise, you'll just end up back in the hospital and you don't want that, do you?"

"God, no!" she pleaded.

"Then I'll see you on Wednesday," I said with a smile.

"Wednesday, it is," she returned with her own smile, baring her enormous teeth. We both stood up to leave and I opened the door for Carrie to walk back into the waiting room.

"Take care," I said as Carrie exited.

When I went back to my desk, I scribbled a few notes about the session.

> *Carrie has a long, hard road ahead of her and I won't be able to be the good guy. She is in desperate need of releasing the anger that's literally eating her body alive. And I will have to be the one to induce her rage.*

I put down my pen and sighed. I'm so tired of that part of the job.

I picked up the phone and called Matt to see what he wanted for dinner. It went to voicemail. He must have been working with some loud machinery at the plant, I figured.

"Hey, Matt, hon, I think I'll run to the store and pick up some steaks for tonight. Call me if you want something else."

Mondays were always slow, particularly in January. The holidays had just passed, which meant most of the family dramas were forgiven or forgotten. It was a new year. A fresh start and it was time for me to get ready for my next session.

# 2

# Jean & Clifford Anderson

Monday January 6th, 2014, Eleventh Session
11:00a.m.

A blinking green light accompanied by a gentle buzzing sound lit up above my desk. Jean and Clifford, or Cliff, as he liked to be called, had arrived and were sitting in the waiting room, undoubtedly giving each other dirty looks. I applied another round of lipstick and checked my hair in the bathroom mirror. Twisting the knob, I opened the door to greet them.

The couple tilted their heads up at me. Both were in their early thirties, very attractive and well-educated. Jean, always anxious for the session, shook my hand with nicely manicured nails to match her purple sweater dress—her long brown hair draped over her shoulder.

Cliff looked debonair as always. He had to take time off work for our session, so he sported business attire with a Santa Claus tie.

"Happy New Year to you both."

"Happy New Year!" they replied together with gleeful looks on their faces.

"Come in, come in," I said. "How were your holidays?" I asked casually while they sat close together on the sofa parallel to me.

"It was very nice, how was yours?" Jean asked.

"I can't complain. Santa stopped by for a quick visit and ate a bunch of my cookies." I smiled to show I was joking. "How are you doing, Cliff?"

"Oh, I'm fine. Yes, we had a lovely Christmas. In fact, the tree is still up. We love it so much, that I don't think we'll take it down for another month." He laughed and looked at his wife. She nodded in agreement.

"So, what's going on now? I feel like it's been forever since I've seen you both. Why was it that you decided to cancel the last two sessions? Was it by choice, or because of money issues?"

Jean pursed her lips and looked straight at the wall. Whenever I mentioned money, she kept her mouth shut. Cliff handled the money issues, so we waited for him to answer. I widened my eyes and gazed at him to nudge him along.

Tension rose and I could tell he was being stubborn. Whenever patients cancelled sessions for more than one week, they had a tendency to slip back into their old habits. It became apparent we had a lot of extra work ahead of us. On the surface, these two could pull off a lovely picture. But I knew that there was a lot of pain and anger lying beneath. Unfortunately, it had to be exposed if they were to make any progress. And this tended to be the messy part of therapy. It's why people stayed away. Problems stayed problems, until someone desired a change. Not to mention, yes, therapy was not cheap. Most health insurance policies didn't allow for it in their plans. If they did, it was usually a limited number of sessions a year. *Hey, is your marriage in trouble? Use the twelve sessions a year we offer, that will fix everything!* It frustrated patients and therapists alike.

"Well, you know. We've begun to pay cash for our sessions and money is always tight around the holidays. Something had to go," Cliff said as he looked at Jean whose face was blank. I felt an argument coming on.

"Why are you looking at me? I wanted to keep the appointments," Jean said.

Cliff threw his arms in the air. "Here we go again!"

"What do you mean? You're blaming me for us not having any money for therapy. That's ridiculous," Jean retorted.

"No, it's not, Jean. In order to pay for dinner with your whole family and my mother, we had to make sacrifices."

I started to watch them like a tennis match.

Nice ace from Cliff.

Jean couldn't return the ball.

He won the point.

Cliff smashed second serve into the net.

Point to Jean.

"Did I say we had to sacrifice therapy?" Jean asked him.

"No, but what else could we have sacrificed? Presents?"

Jean shook her head. "I'm sorry. I should have told everyone to bring something, like a potluck dinner, even though you hate those too."

Cliff bent over and rested his elbows on his knees, then rubbed his face with his hands.

"All right, let's take a break from talking about why you had to cancel two sessions and get back to what we had begun to work on last time, remember what it was?" I laid the challenge at their feet.

"Communication skills and listening?" Jean said uncertainly.

"Yes, did you happen to use any of those tools during the past few weeks?" I gazed at both of them, waiting for an answer. No one spoke. "I guess that would be a no then?"

Cliff and Jean slowly wobbled their heads side to side.

"Then, let's start again." I rose and dragged out my two folding chairs—placing them in the middle of the room. It was apparent that we had some practicing to do and not with tennis. They both huffed and puffed like children as they took their assigned chair, sitting opposite each other. There was a definite amount of steam that needed to be released.

"Ready?" I asked.

"Yes," Jean answered.

"Cliff?"

"Unfortunately, yes," his voice full of sarcasm.

"That's the spirit!" I chirped, ignoring his tone. "Let's pick one feeling." And because I knew they would have fought over a particular feeling before we had even begun, I chose it. "Anger. Cliff, you start, I feel angry at you, Jean—"

He inhaled and said, "I feel angry at you, Jean, because you forget the financial struggles I am under."

"Good, what did you hear Cliff say to you, Jean?" I asked.

"That I'm forgetful and selfish." She sat back and crossed her arms.

"When did I say selfish? Huh? When?" Cliff raged.

"Calm down, calm down. Remember, there is no shouting or name calling." I couldn't for the life of me imagine how they were when no one was around to see them argue. "I didn't hear Cliff say anything about you being selfish. He said forgetful, right, Cliff?"

"Well, if the shoe fits?" he blurted.

It was my turn to throw my hands up into the air.

"How dare you say that to me!" Jean rose to her feet and hovered over Cliff. "I'm the selfish one, yeah? What universe are you living in, huh? Over Christmas, I did the cooking, the cleaning, all the grocery shopping and gift buying." Jean was counting on her fingers as she named off each duty. "What did you do, Cliff? You sat on that goddamn lounge chair with your feet up, drinking Scotch all day long and watching football. You didn't think once about helping me, no." Jean had said her piece. She returned to her chair.

Cliff looked at me and said, "I guess we know what makes Jean angry."

I nodded in agreement with a half-smile. I made a time out signal with my two hands for both of them to see. They turned to face me.

"May I ask, when is the last time you two had sex?"

"About twenty years ago," Cliff chuckled. I laughed too. Jean didn't.

"Why so long? You guys are young, in your thirties, good-looking, healthy, right, Jean?" I gazed her way.

"She doesn't like to have sex with me anymore," Cliff said, gritting his teeth, his smile gone.

"I can speak for myself, thank you very much," Jean said, controlling her anger. She wiped her lower lip with a finger and went back to the couch.

"What's going on, Jean?" I said.

"It's true, we don't have sex anymore. And, honestly, I don't care. Because he comes to bed all liquored up and reeking of cigarettes." Jean continued to stare at me and ignored her husband as if he wasn't even in the room. I gestured for Cliff to sit back on the couch next to Jean and I put away the chairs.

"Cliff, do you think you have a drinking problem?" I asked him directly.

"Yes, he does," Jean said, jumping in the boat and tipping it over.

"I have many problems, and yes, I perhaps drink too much. And smoke too much. But I've never missed a day of work. I put a house over her head and provide money for food and shopping. I would just like to be appreciated by my wife who appears to hate my guts." Cliff's eyes turned glassy which moved Jean to tears.

"I'm sorry, honey, but until you admit you have a problem, we can't be together. I can't predict how you're going to behave from one hour to the next and it scares me. We talked about having kids, remember? For that to happen I have to feel safe with you and right now, I don't."

I allowed Cliff a second to digest what was said. The air in the room could be cut with a knife.

"What are you thinking about right now, Cliff?" I asked.

"I want a divorce." Cliff jumped to his feet and walked toward the door.

"Please stay, Cliff, and finish the session," I begged. "There are other avenues we could try, don't give up yet."

He came back, reached in his back pocket, pulled out his wallet and threw a twenty dollar bill on the couch.

"Here's money for a taxi ride home," he sneered at Jean as he left.

"What on Earth am I going to do now?" Jean asked. She walked around the room shrugging her shoulders, playing the martyr. In reality, she had made a choice for change. The difficult part was living with the consequences.

"You told him how you felt and that's all you can do. I could smell alcohol on him too. So, he's in denial right now. He has to want to change. You can't make him change by withholding sex as a form of punishment."

"I didn't know what else to do." Jean covered her face with her hands and sobbed.

"Please listen to me, Jean. You've planted the seed in him. He now knows why you do what you do. I suggest you go home and give him a little space. His ego has been bruised and exposed. Then, ask him if he wants to talk, and if he does, call me. I'd be happy to schedule you in whenever I can. Until then, I can meet with you one-on-one if you like."

"I don't know if I can afford it," Jean said, laughing and crying at the same time.

"Well, call me and let me know how you're doing either way, all right?"

"Okay." Jean and I walked out to the lounge area where the police guard Ben was stationed.

"Hello, Ms. CarMichael," he said, with a sparkle in his eye.

"Hello, Ben, would you call a taxi for Mrs. Anderson? She needs a ride home."

"Sure thing."

I turned to Jean and said the one thing I could think of saying. "It's not over until it's over."

After she left, I turned to Ben. "That sure wasn't what I expected."

"I saw her husband race down the hall, but since you didn't hit your panic button, I stayed here," Ben said.

"I think their marriage just ended," I said, stretching my arms.

"Oh man! What a great way to start off the year, right?"

"Happy New Year, I want a divorce," I joked.

"Maybe they'll work it out," Ben offered.

"Not unless he quits drinking first." I made a face at Ben. Pretending to be in shock, I placed my hand over my open mouth while I crossed my eyes. "I'm not supposed to be talking about my patients' problems, am I?"

"I'm sorry. I haven't heard a thing you've been talking about. You're kind of boring and ugly. So, I don't pay much attention to you." We both laughed. I turned to walk back to my office, knowing he would be watching me the entire time. I gazed back just to catch him off guard. But it was Ben's smile that got me and a chill went up my spine. We'd been flirting with each other for four years. There was definitely chemistry between the two of us. I usually walked away from his post all gooey inside with my light crush. He made me feel safe. If I had to die, I'd like it to be in his arms. Even though I was dating Matt, this policeman made me feel very special.

"Just another day at the office, right?" I said, loud enough for him to hear.

"Yes, ma'am. You hit that panic button if you need me and I'll come running," Ben teased.

Taking advantage of the early hour, I decided to go shopping. It must have been a busy weekend, because the grocery store was pretty bare. As I wandered down the aisles, customers picked over the shelves, and I saw many disheveled goods placed in the wrong area.

The store was in a recovery mode from the holidays. I grabbed two of the last decent sirloin steaks and a couple of potatoes. I got my usual in the fruit section with the exception of some grapes. I managed to take a handful and place them in my purse. I caught a few people glancing at me and my odd behavior. *I've stolen a handful of grapes—call the fruit police!* My sarcastic inner voice piped up.

On the drive home, I thought of how much I was looking forward to seeing Matt. The sexy nightie I had in the closet from last week's trip to the mall might come in handy. I pulled into my apartment compound and saw Ginger, my striped Bengal cat, by the front door waiting for me.

"Hi, my sweet baby, how was your day?" I said as my cat meowed at me, weaving in and out of my feet. "Oh, come on. I was gone a half-day, you couldn't have missed me too much."

My cell phone rang as I was putting the food in the fridge. I knew it was Matt when his ringtone of "I'm Too Sexy" started playing. I tossed the groceries on the kitchen island so I could reach for my phone.

"Hi, babe," I said. "I'm home early, you ready for some steaks tonight?"

"Oh, sweetie, I took on a double shift. I promised Harry I'd fill in for him as a thank you for last week."

"You could have called me sooner," I said, getting angry. "I went shopping and got all your favorites."

"Calm down, it was a last minute thing. I can come over in the morning," he said, trying to smooth things over.

"Don't bother." I hung up on him. Seething, I placed Ginger's food down on her mat with a fresh bowl of water. I threw the steaks in the fridge and the rest in the pantry. Under the sink, I saw a bottle of Scotch that Matt had left. I grabbed it and a tall glass which was on the counter.

While Ginger was genially eating, I walked over to my sofa and turned the TV on. I filled the glass all the way to the top and began chugging. The liquid burned as it went down my throat and I coughed several times. I was not a big drinker, didn't have what it took to be an alcoholic.

Mind-fucking, now, that was my addiction. But they didn't have twelve-step groups for that, did they? The acid in my stomach added to my irritated mood. But, after a few more sips, all my problems were erased.

*Will & Grace* was playing on TV. Ginger came over and joined me. The episode I was watching had played the same night Matt and I first met. A surge of anger slowly washed over me. I didn't want to be alone tonight. People who have experienced what I had needed a steady relationship. I could take surprises at work. At home, I needed consistency.

I took out the grapes from my purse. Without looking at it, I popped one in my mouth and sucked on its sweet juiciness.

# 3

# Lashanda & Martha Peterson

At work early the next morning, my stomach was aching due to lack of food. To compensate, I had downed two cups of coffee with extra sugar. Trepidation seeped into my thoughts as I realized I had enjoyed eliminating dinner last night. This wasn't normal for me. I didn't ordinarily enjoy suffering. But last night I had. I kept replaying the evening in my head. Just four lousy grapes were sucked upon as the juices dripped down my mouth along with half a bottle of Scotch. Well, to be fair, Matt had drunk most of it a few nights ago. I left the skins of each one of the grapes stuffed inside the bottle of Scotch just to freak Matt out next time he was thirsty.

Mindless, numbing TV was left on until midnight. Even Ginger smelled disgusting to me when she jumped on my lap, purring. The scent of her seafood dinner was still on her whiskers. I felt more powerful as each passing hour went by. It was as if I had accomplished a goal. The weak people needed food. Matt not showing up and making love to me was a gift in disguise. The weak people needed affection. I didn't need him or food. Power was mine to take. No one gives you it. *He had to work a second shift, my ass,* I thought.

Tuesday January 7ᵗʰ, 2014, Lashanda & Martha Peterson, Tenth Session 10:00a.m.

The waiting room light flashed green and I took a huge breath. I was definitely not in the mood for the mother and daughter bang-up, drag-down, beat-the-crap-out-of-each-other duo. Suddenly, an idea came to me: *let's see which one of them wins today.* If there was no restraining coming from me, would they continue on their usual course of action? I knew of course they would. Even if a miracle was to come down from God, it would merely slow them down. I had become a referee in a boxing match. I had pressed my panic button every time the two of them graced my room.

Lashanda was fifteen and already had been in numerous fights, kicked out of two different schools and had five run-ins with the law. She was tall, husky and had a sailor's mouth on her. Poor impulse control ran in the family, as her mother blatantly displayed the exact same tendencies. The state was picking up the tab for their therapy as with many of my patients. (Insurance doesn't pay shit even though they are required to by law.) To be fair, they couldn't afford insurance premiums anyway. Being poor isn't a crime, but being violent with zero impulse control is. So, the three of us were stuck with each other for the time being.

Apprehension filled my mind as I went out to greet them. This dreadful pattern appeared when they were on my schedule. Martha was all smiles as she jumped up to shake my hand—dressed in a yellow blouse and jeans. When I got a whiff of her, I was bombarded with twenty ounces of perfume. I had to choke back a cough.

"How are you today, Ms. CarMichael?" she asked with her usual enthusiasm.

"I'm fine and yourself?"

"Busy, so busy, traffic was so bad I didn't think we'd make it on time." Martha stopped speaking and looked down at Lashanda, who was stoic. "What's the matter with you? Stand up and say hello properly to Ms. CarMichael right now." Martha slapped Lashanda's head for her indolent behavior.

*And we are officially off to the races, ladies and gentlemen!*

Lashanda shot her mother an angry look and then her eyes glanced toward me. Usually, I would interrupt their exchange, but I did nothing to throw them off-kilter.

"Shall we go in?" I asked, motioning to my door. Lashanda stood to reveal her pink shorts and white jacket she had zipped up to her neck. For a second, I wondered if she had anything tucked in there. Kids, noticeably ones from her neighborhood, carried weapons. Therapists were not immune to these nefarious situations (panic button). Her jet-black hair was tightly whipped into a ponytail, identical to her mother's.

Once in my office, the mother and daughter sat on opposite sides of the couch. I adjusted the thermostat to make the room warmer before I took my place at the desk. This was the best method of getting vulpine teenagers to reveal whether or not they had weapons tucked under their clothes.

"So, how are things going?" I asked, getting out my notebook and pen.

"Do you want to tell her, or should I?" Martha asked her daughter. Lashanda shrugged her shoulders and lowered her head.

"Answer me! Don't just sit there like a lump." Martha's eyes widened as I saw her getting angrier by the minute. Meanwhile, Lashanda's head swayed back and forth. Her derogatory eyes snidely glanced in her mother's direction. It was five minutes into the session and already I predicted fireworks on the horizon. I kept the panic button in my vision and dropped my notepad—placing my pen in my drawer. It was never a good idea to have sharp objects lying around with these two.

"All right, I got in another fight," Lashanda admitted.

Martha looked triumphantly at me and lifted up her hands. I promptly ignored her. Again, my inauspicious plan was to stay neutral and see what happened. With each passing second I didn't feel we'd have a favorable outcome, but was convinced there had to be a better way.

"So what's going on at home?" I asked instead, with my head down, looking at the carpet, so neither one of them would know who the question was for. It's a tactic I used when working with more than one person in a session. Everything told me something, who answered and who was quiet. My favorite was when they both answered at the same time.

"Nothing out of the usual." Martha spoke first.

"And what is the *usual* these days, Martha?"

"Oh, you know, just trying to make a living and holding down two jobs. My husband comes and goes when he wants. He's no good for the kids because he's drunk all the time." Martha's nostrils flared as her breathing became taxing, and noticeably louder. She was working herself up into a violent frenzy.

"After he leaves, I have to do damage control. He makes things chaotic, unstable, you know," Martha said, beginning to sweat.

"What do you mean by chaotic?" I asked.

"Well, he doesn't change the baby. He cooks and refuses to clean the dishes. And he invites his so-called friends over to play cards when I'm at work. I come home to a filthy house, smelling like a chimney, a screaming baby and toys and dishes everywhere. He lets the kids do whatever they want!" Martha crossed her arms and leaned back.

"That does sound chaotic," I agreed.

"And instead of Lashanda helping me out with her younger siblings, she's making me run to the school practically every day." Martha exhaled and threw her hands up once again.

"Lashanda, how do you feel when your dad is home?" I adjusted my head to see Lashanda's face.

"I don't know," she said. Her lips pressed tightly together as she ran her thumb over them, her fists clenched.

Getting Lashanda to discuss her feelings was like trying to make iced tea without boiling water. Next to impossible. Sure, you could place it out in the hot sun for hours. But that took time and patience. A person could say the same thing about Lashanda.

"It has to be hard to have all that responsibility put on you, huh?" I engaged.

"Uh huh," Lashanda whispered.

"When I was fifteen, all I wanted was to fit in at school and feel safe at home. But, it doesn't look like you have that option, Lashanda. Would you agree?"

"Yeah."

"So you fight to get your mom's attention, to feel safe and try to tell her you don't like all this responsibility."

"Maybe." Lashanda lifted her head.

"What do you mean, maybe? Are you saying I'm the one to blame?" Martha didn't like what she was hearing. She looked at me and back to her daughter. I allowed the significance to gnaw at her. Lashanda unzipped her jacket and threw me a grin. I needed to reward this action.

"Be careful, Lashanda," I said. "If you keep smiling, people might start thinking something is wrong with you," I teased. An endearing snicker escaped from Lashanda as she covered her mouth with her hand and peered at her mother.

"Why did you do that? Why did you cover up your laugh?" I asked sincerely.

"I don't know," she said.

"I didn't know she could laugh," Martha added. As soon as the words came out of her mother's mouth Lashanda turned serious again. Her jaw clenched shut. It might not have ever been easy for Lashanda to verbalize what she was feeling, but, boy she could show it.

"So, what I hear you saying Martha, is, if you can't be happy, then no one else should be allowed to be happy either. Correct?" I confronted Martha for berating her daughter. She had been doing this from our first day of therapy. Even though I continued to trample on her when she made comments like those, Martha refused to concede.

"Did I say that? No! I did not. You're putting words into my mouth," Martha lashed out at me. Standing up, confusing both of them, I went to one of my bookshelves that had wooden blocks of feeling words printed on them, like: 'sad', 'happy' and 'worry'. I grabbed the one that said 'happy' and brought it over to Martha.

"Open wide," I said to the mother.

"What? Lady, you done gone nuts," Martha said, failing to get the joke. However, Lashanda did and began a cackle, which made my day. Her body rocked back and forth as she shook with laughter.

"You said I was putting words into your mouth. So, I was just following your lead," I joked, winking at Lashanda.

"But, you're say'n that *I'm* the one with the problem, right?" Martha raised her voice and glared back at me. It was time for me to lighten the mood.

"We've all got problems, Martha. The point is to try not to take yourself and your problems so seriously all the time," I said with a nod. Martha eyed me for an instant. Thinking I had made my point, I returned to my desk and sat down.

A long drawn out pause followed and I felt like a bomb was ticking. Martha sneered at me the entire time. She tilted her head away and dismissed me with a wave of her hand.

"It must be easy for you to sit there and make fun of me," Martha said.

"I wasn't making fun of you. I was trying, I guess unsuccessfully, to make a point," I said, raising my voice an octave. Muscles tightened in both my shoulders and I sat up straight. I didn't like being bullied. Who did?

"Yes, you were making fun of me," she wrinkled her nose and snorted. "You sit here in your nice office with your pretty clothes with all your money. I bet you feel safe! I bet you don't worry about your crazy-ass daughter fightin' all the time!" Martha stood, walked over to me and I leaned backward, clutching my chest. The old fight or flight thoughts went spinning in my head. For some reason, I couldn't see my panic button.

"Please sit down. We don't scream in our sessions." But it was no use. Martha's rage went from zero to ten in less than a second. Her full-rage mode was on and ready with her fists clenched, bosom perched. The first swing came from my right side. I dodged it just in the nick of time. Martha made contact with the desk lamp instead. I ducked under my desk and peeked out around the edge to see Lashanda approaching, coming to my rescue. The two of them threw punches and yanked at each other's nice and tidy ponytails. I skirted around them and crawled on my hands and knees out of the office. Once in the waiting room, I rose to my feet and tore down the hall.

"Security, help!" I screamed, feeling somewhat mischievous. Had my plan worked? I had intervened a little but it didn't quell their violent behavior. And as for who won the fight? I guess we'd find out.

The officer on duty—Ben—was running in my direction. His broad shoulders moved, swaying with his hips. Mmm, I adored his short curly red hair.

"What's wrong?" he said.

"You might need back-up, two patients are fighting in my office," I said, trying to catch my breath. God, I needed to get in better shape. And maybe even start classes in self-defense. I'd heard that Ben and his friends traded off teaching classes at night. It would be a perfect opportunity to kill two birds with one stone. I could indulge with my little crush on Ben and learn a few self-defense moves at the same time. Bingo!

"Oh, crap," he said and called on his shoulder phone. "Officer needs assistance with therapist's patients, room 254." The building that held my office was next to the major hospital in central Florida and always had plenty of police nearby.

"Thanks, I didn't even have time to hit my panic button. The mother clambered after me and the daughter went to defend me, or at least that's what I think happened. I got out of there fast."

Ben moved a little closer to me as he received an update. Apparently there was some sort of trouble in the ER next door and they were busy restraining people, so it would be a few minutes before they could send reinforcements.

Huge clanging noises came from down the hall inside my office and a feeling of panic washed over me. I was beginning to regret antagonizing Martha. I had a sudden urge to run to my car and just go home. Ben looked the opposite. Though he was going to wait for back-up, I saw his eyes fixated on my office door. His posture remained sturdy, chin high and shoulders squared.

There was a wonderful smell of oranges that came from his body. It must have been his aftershave, but to me, it smelled like sex. Suddenly, I had the urge to lick his neck, but resisted the temptation.

"I guess I'm going solo on this one." Ben initiated moving in the direction of the screaming.

"No. I don't want you to. Those two are very violent." I reached out and held his arm in protest.

Sounds of breaking glass echoed down the hall, coming from my room. I heard one of them screech. I'd never heard a sound like that from a human being before. There were more crashes and the sound of splintering wood. Mother and daughter had crossed over to the indomitable stage.

"Maybe you'd better," I said with a nervous smile.

"Yeah," Ben laughed and guardedly jogged toward my office.

"Just don't taser them, please!" I begged. "Oh, and grab my purse if you can." The stupidity of my last statement surprised even me. Ben ceased moving, pivoted around to gaze at me, and then he chuckled. I placed my hands in my side pockets and shrugged my shoulders. I watched as he disappeared into my office.

Chaotic noises followed as my patients now realized the police were involved. I decided to approach as I heard accusations go around the room as to whose fault it was that this had happened.

By the time I reached my office door, all was quiet, and I peered in to see that Ben had them calm and restrained on the floor by one of the couches with their hands handcuffed behind them. The room was a fucking mess. Broken picture frames and cracked shelves were strewed across the office. It would take forever to clean up. Then the thought came to me, *why even bother to tidy it?* So they can just do it again? It was so frustrating. When Ben moved away, I saw the mother and daughter's faces. Martha's eyes were bright, jovial even. Lashanda was grinning first, then her smile disappeared and she tilted her head lower when she saw my expression. The two of them now acted sweet as candy. It took every ounce of strength for me to not go over and smack the shit out of them. I decided that would add to the bloodstain that was tarnishing the carpet. Thank you very much.

"You can come in," Ben said signaling me with his hand. I gingerly approached and tried to force a gentle look of concern on my face, but really I was pissed.

"Are we all good now?" I asked, not caring for their answers.

"Yes," mother and daughter said in unison. Fucking crazy bitches.

"Would you like to press charges against these two?" Ben directed his question at me.

I pondered the correct amount of time to let them both sweat about it. But even that didn't work. Because they knew the system. They knew how everything would go down. They were on welfare and had no money, so they would keep taking it out on innocent people until one of them went too far and ended up in prison. I was sick of all of this.

"No, I won't press any charges. But I will not be your therapist any longer." They hunched their heads over as if they were devastated, but I knew they couldn't care less. "Please escort them out of the building," I said. Just then, two other officers appeared.

"How we doing?" asked the short, plump one, called James. The other one I didn't know, but he was taller than Ben. I felt safer. All three men helped Lashanda and Martha Peterson stand up and exit the building in an orderly fashion. Mother and daughter were no longer my patients, but I'd be dealing with their parting gifts for quite some time. I heard the door close behind them and the scent of oranges left a trail hanging in the air. I returned to my office and locked the door.

I picked up what I could off the floor. Saving all the toys and puzzles, I put them in the basket. My family photo that I kept on my desk was shattered. Tiny pieces of glass covered the surrounding area. It was the one decent picture I had of my dad. Simply another victim lost in the hurricanes called Martha and Lashanda. That's what these people were: disasters. They were unpredictable and capable of destroying things of sentimental value—because to them, nothing *had* any value. They were sociopaths. I sat at my desk, exhausted, and called the maid service for the building. I told them I needed a new carpet and hung up. I covered my face with both hands and started to sob. My chest ached as I lightly brushed over the broken picture frame of my family.

# 4

# Even Therapists Need Therapy

After three hours of cleaning and reorganizing my office, I noticed I'd let the time slip through my fingers. My shrink, Dr. Sharon Hingley, was wondering what happened to me. Shrinks needed shrinks too. This was something most people didn't know. In order for me to be licensed in the state of Florida and keep my insurance rates low, I had to have sessions with her. It also kept my sanity intact, even though in that space, it appeared to be spiraling down the drain at a rapid pace.

Dr. Sharon Hingley owned the company I worked for, and made referrals to me. I had to report to her on a regular basis. Plus, a little incident of mine that happened seven years ago meant I had to oblige with seeing a shrink. If I wanted to continue any sort of practice, this was the deal. Technically, she was a psychiatrist and could prescribe medication. I couldn't. I had completed my Master's degree in Social Work with an emphasis on therapy. I attempted to get my doctorate, but life got in the way. I had to think of it as a sponsor from one of those twelve-step programs.

Even though I disliked my sponsor immensely and she wasn't all touchy-feely for me, either.

I grabbed my coat because it was freezing outside, by Floridian standards, anyway. I placed my tennis shoes on and jogged, all the while thinking at least I would have lots of issues to bring to the table today. Luckily, her office was just a few buildings down in the same complex. The sky was overcast and trees were bare. I hated winter time. Leaf blowers swerved in and out of the street. The noises added to my irritation.

My jogging slowed down as I got closer to her building. Twenty-four floors and her office was on the top floor. I fanned myself off in the women's bathroom, fixing my hair and wiping off the smeared make-up from my hissy fit. There was always a stretch I dreaded when I entered her waiting room. To say that jealousy consumed me would be an understatement. I felt tiny. Her waiting room alone was three times larger than mine, with fresh flowers and soothing new age music. It didn't help matters either that she consistently made me wait, even when I was on time, and I knew she had no other clients before me. She pressed my buttons. I was thirty years old and I would regress whenever we had a session. The pleasure I took from the situation was the knowledge that she had to see a shrink too. Covering your ass, as well as your associates' asses was paramount in this field. I wondered how high up the hierarchy went.

Contemplating my day so far, I decided there would be a pile of bullshit for her to dig through before I would come to mention the boxing match between mother and daughter. While Sharon loved digging into messy sessions such as the one I'd just experienced, I lacked enthusiasm. My stomach digested much better with non-violent chit-chat. I had to watch my pace so she wouldn't pick up on any clues.

Side-stepping issues was something I had developed quite a knack for. Me? Oh, I'm fine. Patients were doing their homework. They're learning to use words and not their fists. My love-life was spectacular. I'm not attracted at all to having a possible affair with Ben the cop. Every time I smelled oranges I wanted to come. My proverbial sarcasm knew no limits.

"Lindsey, are you ready?" Dr. Sharon Hingley made her grand entrance. The psychiatric world was a stage and the center light beamed for her. She reminded me of Scarlett from *Gone with the Wind*. I couldn't remember how many times I'd wanted to end our sessions with: "Frankly, my dear, I don't give a damn..."

The measly pleasure I took in working under her, was that I had been the one to originally suggest she proceed with a private practice—in a sleight of hand way. And she had never even thanked me for it, imagine that?

"Hi, Dr. Hingley, how are you?" I said, with my typical cheerful tone as I avoided eye contact and entered the room. I gritted my teeth as silently as possible. Never once had she suggested for me to call her by her first name. I looked around her office, which was pristine perfect as usual. Not a thing was out of place, there were three couches, two throw rugs, one central station where she kept her laptop, notepad and a place to swipe your credit cards. This came complete with a laser printout for receipts attached to it. On more than one occasion I'd been tempted to write in a tip just to see what she would do. There were live plants everywhere, including moth orchids, a money tree, zebra plants and of course a lucky bamboo. Her pictures all reflected the plants. So, basically you felt like you were in a fucking jungle. I made a face at the fake lizards beneath the plants, but they didn't respond. I avoided looking at her wall of fame, where she had her degrees and accolades in golden frames above her station. Obviously, so she could glance up at them and pat herself on the back every hour. Good therapist.

"Have a seat. I'll be with you in just a minute," Sharon told me as she opened her laptop and typed a cool sixty-words-per-minute. Making me wait was all part of her routine. The bitch. I stared at the white orchids and counted. Three minutes was her usual setting-up time. Don't get me wrong, I do this with my patients too. I just hate it when it's done to me. I crossed my legs and closed my eyes.

"Are you tired today?" she asked.

"Oh, I'm sorry. I had a bit of a rough day," I said. Dammit! She caught me off guard. *Had I dozed off for a second?* Sharon was now sitting facing me with her judgmental expression, making me feel uncomfortable.

"Really? Tell me about it," she said.

"It was nothing. Just a typical session with Martha and Lashanda getting into an altercation during their session." Fuck! Fuck! I wanted to play this down. Sharon's eyes lit up. She smelled blood. I focused on the orchid again and tried to slow my breathing. Faking a yawn, I stretched out my arms.

"You *are* tired, aren't you?" she asked.

"Just a little. Matt and I had a fight last night and I didn't sleep *(or eat)* very much." Leave it to a therapist to know how to change the subject. A skill developed with training through many years of listening to patients who are unwilling to express their feelings.

"What was it about?"

"I called him when I got home," I exhaled, "and he said he took on an extra shift for one of his friends. So he wasn't able to come over for dinner."

My therapist nodded her head, but made no sound. I hated when she did that. When I let another few minutes go by, she waved her hand like I was a trained dog. She needed a little more explanation. (And how did that make you feel, you pathetic excuse for a human being?)

"Okay! I was pissed. I had gotten off work early and bought his favorite food and really wanted to get laid, happy?"

Nothing. I wanted to inflict bodily harm on this woman.

"The truth is," I said, finding myself opening up, when really I wanted to run away, "Matt and I have started drifting apart."

"What makes you think that?" she asked.

"It's the way he's been talking to me lately. I feel like I'm not that important to him anymore. I'm not number one, you know?"

"Have you talked to him about this?"

"No," I said and fixated on the white leaves on the orchid.

"Maybe he's going through a difficult time or something is bothering him. You'll never know until you ask."

"I know, I know." I didn't need to be talked down to like I was a teenager. God, I hated coming here.

"You sound like you're getting defensive, Lindsey. I'm asking questions because it's my job and frankly, you look stressed and unhappy. Am I right?" Sharon leaned in on her chair toward me, looking happy with herself.

I wanted to throw the planted orchid at her head. *Where were all these violent thoughts coming from? Oh yeah, the gang fight I was witness to by mother and daughter of the year. Shit like that tended to rub off on you.*

"Maybe you're right. I am a little off-kilter today. I didn't mean to take it out on you."

"That's what I'm here for; to advise you and see if I can help." She sparkled her fake smile at me. Her eyes radiated a dominant glare. No wonder she had someone pull a gun on her during her session.

"You do help. And because I see what you're getting at, I've decided to take some time and rest. You know? Really find out where I'm going with Matt and rejuvenate, recommit or whatever I need to do. Sound good?"

I looked over at her and she began to fidget with her ten-thousand dollar diamond bracelet. This meant she wasn't happy. She swallowed hard to clear her throat. Sharon turned toward her desk and started writing on a notepad. That could mean one thing.

"Not quite sure this is the time for all that. I have a new referral for you."

"Dr. Hingley, I don't know if I want to take on another case right now. If anything, I love my schedule the way it is. God, I need a vacation."

"Vacation?" Her jaw clenched and she kept scratching the back of her neck. I had noticed this was something she did when she was having trouble finding the right words to say.

"Yes, vacation. I haven't been on one for over two years and I'm getting burned out." I played over in my mind several different scenarios she'd come up with to counter me, but she stuck with the new referral.

"Well, all right then, I'll take him. I just thought his issues were right up your alley, so to speak." Sharon spoke rapidly. She was used to getting her way. She began to crumple up the piece of paper she was going to give me.

"Wait, wait, what's the case?"

"Male, age sixteen, antisocial, loner, you name it. His parents are very worried he's depressed. At least his mother is, I couldn't get a decent vibe off of his father. I think their marriage is in trouble." Sharon sat back, crossing her arms and moving her chin up.

"Why do you think this is right up my alley?" I couldn't fathom. It didn't make sense.

"Really? Carrie Warner sounds similar to him. In that they are both dealing with adolescent issues."

"Also sounds a little like my case with Milo Cooper," I added.

"Milo is a self-loathing, neurotic, pussy-whipped little boy in a man's body," she said as if it were a fact.

My jaw dropped open. I almost fell off of the sofa. I had been having sessions with Dr. Hingley for three years and never once had she sworn in front of me—let alone said 'pussy'. Sharon raised her eyebrows and sat back in her chair. "I should not have said that," she said with a grin.

"No, well, you were spot-on though. I will give you that." I returned. And we both had a hearty chuckle for a few minutes. Nice to know she was nowhere near perfect either.

Then she got serious again. We both did. No one enjoyed being dictated to, especially therapists. Ruminating for a little while, I decided it was time for me to tell her. I took a deep breath in and exhaled. I knew my plate wasn't exactly full at that time, but I liked it that way. As long as I had enough funds to pay my bills, I was happy with my light workload.

"Has he been in therapy before?" I asked.

"No." Sharon leaned, advancing in her chair with narrowed eyes. "Do you want him or not?" She swung the paper as if it were a carrot dangling over me. I swear to God, the woman had no shame.

"I need to find him a place on my schedule. I assume he's in school and the parents both work?" I said, sliding my tongue slowly along the inside of my cheek while waiting for her to answer. For some reason, whenever I came here, I couldn't get the muscles in my face and jaw to relax.

"Mother is a secretary and dad is a car salesman. Time of day might not be an issue at all. If that's what you're worrying about." Sharon smugly rested her chin on her hand. "But, the client is the boy. He's in school. I'm sure he could come for a session immediately after, around three. His mother will take time off if necessary."

I sighed. That wasn't what I was worried about. Time of day didn't bother me. Not having time off did. *Bitch*. She always had to win.

"Yes, I'll take him. Is that everything?" The longer I stayed, the harder it was to remain civil. It seemed I wouldn't be getting a vacation any time soon after all.

"Maybe he likes to play with toys too," I said under my breath. I felt my pulse rise.

"I beg your pardon?" she snapped.

"Nothing," I said, shaking my wrists until I calmed down. Sharon dismissed this action as a tick of some sort, or so she had told me many times.

I stood up and walked over to get the new client's information. Sharon studied my appearance and I wondered if she was having second thoughts about giving me a new client. Good. I enjoyed keeping her on her toes. At least I'd said for the record that I was burned out and needed a holiday. She would be more than responsible if my deck of cards fell down.

"Are you sure you want to take this on?"

"I am." This time, it was me who snapped. Sharon looked puzzled with her insincere (what have I done wrong now?) look. She adjusted herself in leather-back chair and decided to push my buttons. I started to head for the door.

"Lindsey, your session is not over. We still have twenty minutes." Sharon pointed to her watch with a smile.

"Oh, I wasn't thinking straight." I laughed. My therapist didn't. I went over to the biggest sofa and sat with my legs tucked up beside me. I half wanted to take a nap.

"Tell me about this little altercation you had with Martha and Lashanda." My therapist knew the tricks too.

5

# A Surprise Waiting at Home

By the time I drove home, I was thoroughly exhausted from the day's events. I had supervised the installation of my new office carpet. A warm shade of mauve now graced the office floor, erasing all signs of the violent struggle. Sharon was appalled when I told her what had occurred. She told me I could also pick out some new furniture, and bill it to the company. I think she felt guilty denying my request for a holiday. Whatever it was, I took it.

I caught myself spacing out driving home on Interstate 95 Highway, which was not a good idea. Flashing images of punches being thrown and broken glass shattered all my senses. It was signs of PTSD. I'd hidden it well for the past seven years and would continue to do so until they locked me up. Most therapists had it, or so I chose to believe. And they would point out that it came with the territory.

I breathed out a huge sigh of relief when I got to my exit. All I wanted to do was go home and crash for the night. No crazy people allowed. My heart sank when I pulled into the complex. Matt's car was in my driveway. He was parked in front of the apartment and had all the lights on inside my place. I heard the TV blaring some stupid sports game from inside my apartment. He had the windows wide open in the kitchen so I knew the whole neighborhood could hear.

"Wonderful," I said out loud as I got out the car and slammed my door shut. For some reason, I didn't want to see him. I knew he'd want to hear all the gritty details of my work (which he always laughed about). He thoroughly enjoyed the craziness that I had to put up with on a per diem. At times, it was more entertaining for him than football. Then, I would be forced to listen to his bullshit stories from his forklifting buddies at the plant. Which guy was screwing some model from Miami or who got a low score mark on their performance record. As I got out of my car, I heard the front door open.

"Here she is, Ginger," he said to my cat who was in his arms, forcing her to wave a paw hello. She twisted herself out of his grip and dropped to the ground. Even Ginger wasn't in the mood for him tonight.

"Did she scratch you?" I inquired, walking up the steps.

"No, but she tried. I learned my lesson from last time." He laughed and stretched his arms wide open to embrace me. I willingly obliged with a grin and closed my eyes. He kissed my cheek and I brushed my hand through his balding dark hair. He stank of grease and sweat from head to toe. It permeated through his clothes. "And since I ruined last night's dinner, I brought home

Chinese takeout. Honey garlic chicken!" he said, acting like he wanted a gold star. My hero.

"Hmm...Sounds great, babe. I'm so tired. Come on, Ginger." I coaxed her to come inside with us. "Just let me feed her first and—
—"

As I stepped into the kitchen, Matt pushed me against the fridge and began kissing the back of my neck while reaching around me. He placed one hand straight between my legs and the other one went from breast to breast, gripping them roughly. I gasped, trying to catch my breath.

"Matt, wait!" I said. But he didn't, and after a few seconds, I gave in to it. He took me right there and then against the cold metal. And despite my initial protests, I realized that I wanted it too. He undid my pants and his, and forced his way inside. He pulled my hair, tilting my head back so he could put his thumb in my mouth. I sucked it hard and he moaned, which made him thrust harder. With every thrust, I could feel myself responding, lubricating our brutish coupling. He rubbed my clitoris and I moaned loudly, I was so close to coming. His thrusts increased in speed and depth and I gripped onto the kitchen counter as we came together. He kept rubbing me and I enjoyed several more waves while he slowed down. Matt released his grip on me slowly, out of breath.

"That felt so good, babe," he whispered and pulled up his jeans.

Legs trembling, I had to admit it did feel good. But it bothered me that there was an aggressive and detached feeling in his actions.

Where had our emotional connection gone? Had we even had one in the first place? He'd been raring to go before I'd even walked in the door. I didn't look glamorous for Christ-sake. Drained from the day, I decided to let it go. The last thing I needed tonight was another confrontation.

"Well, you did buy the Chinese, so I guess you deserved a quickie," I giggled. I poured myself a drink, needing a few minutes to recover. Matt didn't. Having his first thirst sated, Matt dove straight into stage two, the food. He ate like a pig, getting most of the contents on his shirt. I began to see him through Carrie Warner's eyes and lost my appetite.

"I'll be right back," I said, excusing myself. I went into the bedroom. I wanted to take a nice hot bath, but knew that would trigger Matt's need for another round. As I removed my clothes, I saw bruises on my knees and my cheekbone was sore. The first was from crawling out of the battlefield this morning. The second was from my loving boyfriend making love to me by pushing my face against the fridge. Yeah, this needed to end. I put on the ugliest robe I had and went back to the kitchen.

When I returned to the kitchen, I saw Matt staring out the front window with interest. Slowly creeping up behind him, I wondered what had caught his attention. Then I noticed a parked car when I leaned over his shoulder. It was sitting precisely adjacent from my building. Matt peeked over his shoulder at me.

"I hate that robe. Are you expecting anyone?"

"No, who is it?" I pushed myself closer to the window to get a better look. The beige car took off, speeding down the road. "What kind of car was that?" I asked him.

"A Chrysler, looks like a...I don't know, one of their newer models maybe," he said, while shaking his head. "I don't know." He shrugged his shoulders and grabbed a beer out of the fridge.

"So, what you're saying is you don't know? Correct?" Sarcasm was always my first weapon of choice.

"Smartass, no, I don't. You made your point."

"It has to be one of my patients who've decided to stalk me. Give them a few minutes and they'll get bored to tears and go rob a convenience store instead," I joked, but Matt appeared uninterested.

"Don't worry about it, sweetie," he said, slugging down his beer.

"Oh, believe me, I'm not worried. My patients are all too busy taking their aggression out on themselves. I don't think they give me a second thought once they leave my office. But, hey, thanks for your concern." Sarcasm dripped from every word which caused Matt to grimace in discontentment. My sense of humor was usually lost on him.

"I didn't say I wasn't concerned, Lindsey. Would you please just sit down and eat some dinner? Don't worry about whoever is in that car. They're just lost or took a wrong turn or something."

"All right, let me get Ginger's dinner and then I'll have a bite." By the time I set the dish of cat food in front of Ginger and put some Chinese food on a plate, Matt had already finished eating and was watching a war movie on TV.

This was our typical nightly routine I had gotten used to. He fucked me quick, we drank and ate and watched some TV. I enjoyed watching comedies like *Will & Grace*, but of course he thought it was lame, which I found ironic because the show had been playing on TV the night we first met at a party. He had approached me with his witty charm and pretended to be a fan of the show after witnessing how much it made me laugh. These days, it was all war and football. The charm and wit were long gone.

I curled up on the couch and ate my chicken. It was the first meal I had eaten in two days. I gave Ginger some scraps because she wouldn't leave me alone and then she went to my bedroom. I glanced at Matt, and saw his eyes were half shut.

"You want to go to bed?" I asked.

He jumped at my voice and I started to laugh. "Jesus!"

"I'm sorry, I didn't mean to scare you." I giggled some more which did not bode well for me. "Baby, come on. Get your ass in my room and sleep."

Matt threw his legs up and stretched, placing one hand on my head. He patted me like a little kid.

"Are you going to come with me? You know how scared I get sleeping alone." He made a baby face with pouting lips.

"Aw…I hear some bullshit approaching," I sighed.

"Please come and protect me. I'll be a good boy, I promise."

Even though I knew he just wanted to have sex again, I decided to take him up on his offer.

"Well, hell, anything is more comfortable than the refrigerator." I smiled.

He smiled back and held out his hand to me.

We managed to go another round in bed. This time, he was gentler with me. I faked it this time, too tired for another orgasm. Matt drifted off to sleep and I showered and slipped into my favorite pajamas. Ginger tried to sleep by my side but got fed up of my fidgeting. She jumped off the bed and went out of the room. She probably had to take a piss and I kept her box in the laundry room. Matt's snoring caused me to nudge him several times. I didn't sleep well at all. Each time I glanced over to the clock, another hour had passed by. It was as if I had been floating. The images which appeared to me in my dreams kept me from getting a good night's sleep.

A gloomy feeling came upon me as the clock turned to 6:00 a.m. My cell phone rang. I reached over and grabbed it.

"Hello? My name is Anna and I work at the Sunny Beaches Animal Clinic. Who am I speaking to?" a female on the other end asked.

"This is Lindsey CarMichael."

"Do you own a cat named Ginger?"

Sitting up in bed, I nudged Matt with my hand. My breathing quickened.

"Yes, I have a cat named Ginger," I said, glaring over at Matt. He blinked sleepily, and rubbed his eyes.

"I'm sorry to alarm you, but we have her here down at the Sunny Beaches Animal Clinic. She was brought here by the police and we saw your number on her collar tag."

"Oh my God! Is she okay?" Jumping out of bed, I began to pace back and forth.

"Not really. It looks like someone intentionally hurt her. She has several burn marks that we are attending to now."

"No!" The room began to spin and things went out of focus.

"What the hell is happening?" Matt was now fully awake.

I covered the receiver and whispered. "Ginger got outside during the night and somebody hurt her. She's at the animal clinic."

"How did she get out?" Matt looked puzzled.

I waved my hand to tell him to shut up. "Is she going to be all right?" Afraid to hear the answer, I covered my eyes with my spare hand.

"There's more. I'm afraid whoever hurt her also stabbed her in the eye with a carved out stick. We need your permission to operate on her as soon as possible. Because, it looks like the object went through her pupil destroying her retina. She won't be able to see in her left eye anymore."

"Oh my God," I cried. "Yes, you have my permission to operate and I'll be right there." My stomach knotted. I began to feel lightheaded. I was either going to puke or pass out.

"Thank you and we are very sorry," she said.

Hanging up the phone, I fought back the urge to be sick and ran to get dressed as Matt followed me, asking questions. I told him all I knew and said I'd call him later. He was as upset as I was. Neither one of us could figure out how she got outside. I had closed all the windows in the apartment after supper, hadn't I? The last time I saw her was when she had jumped off the bed. She never did come back. Too wrapped up in my restless sleep, I didn't notice her absence. How did she get outside? And who would want to hurt her?

All these thoughts swam around my mind as I jumped in my car and drove to the clinic. The parking lot outside of the plain brown, one-story building was empty due to the early hour. Cold and rainy weather accompanied me as I slid out of the car. I got sick to my stomach thinking that she'd spent the entire night in this horrible climate and been attacked as well.

"I'm Lindsey CarMichael, you have my cat Ginger," I said, charging into the waiting area. My voice was full of desperation as I grabbed hold of the countertop for support where a nurse stood behind. My knees still shook.

A towering blonde with her hair pulled back said, "Yes, come this way." She opened the hallway door and led me into the clinic. Brightly lit rooms greeted my non-caffeinated state of mind. I was running on pure adrenaline. The doctor, who sported tiny glasses, long white over coat and gloved hands, greeted me.

"I'm Dr. Goldman, Ginger is fine and resting," he said removing his gloves. He steadily approached me. His voice had a soothing tone, which made me think the situation was worse than they said on the phone.

"Okay," I said, clearing my throat.

"We performed surgery and removed the object from her eye. In addition, we treated several of her wounds."

"She's not in any pain, is she?" My heartbeat raced listening to him.

"No, she's still in recovery and will have to stay here for a few days. Have you seen any animals abused before?" he asked.

"Yes, on those dreadful TV commercials they play when you least expect it. I usually have to change the channel fast before I begin to cry." I choked down a sobbing sound.

"Many people feel that way. It is very upsetting to watch. Believe me, I know. And it will be difficult for you to see her. I want you to know that before I take you in. A commercial is one thing, but you won't be able to change the channel once you walk inside." His eyes remained steady and direct.

"I understand," I said, tears running down my cheeks.

"The unusual thing about this attack was the object we removed from her eye..." he hesitated. Dr. Goldman's facial expression was grave as he sat quietly on a stool with his hands folded.

I thought I was going to have a heart attack on the spot.

He straightened his shoulders back and said it. "The object which the attacker used to blind your cat appeared to be a hand-carved stake made of ginger root."

I frowned at the absurdity of his words. "A what?"

"I know it's bizarre, we were baffled at first too, but when we analyzed it, that's what it seemed to be, a piece of ginger root with a fine, sharp point."

"So, that means..." My legs went like rubber and Dr. Goldman caught me just as I was about to fall. I tried to scream but nothing came out. Instead, I started crying, blubbering nonsensical words. He and his staff gave me some water and tried to allay my fears as I sat on a warm chair. After a few minutes, rocking back and forth, my hunched over posture straightened even though I kept my arms wrapped around each other. I calmed down and my mind flooded with questions.

"Whoever did this, they must have known her name, right?" I asked.

"Yes. It is written on her collar tag. I do agree that this appears to be pre-meditated with the stick. I've already placed a call for the police to come back and do a full report. They couldn't say the exact time they'd return, but assured me it would be today. Do you feel well enough to see her now?"

I nodded yes and then dragged my feet as I followed him. He took me to a dimly-lit room and I saw my baby. My hands flew to my chest. The room had a slightly acrid smell. I became light-headed and I had to remind myself to breathe. Her striped fur was tangled from top to bottom. An IV was attached to her front paw. Her head was methodically bandaged up except for her one good eye. It was difficult to see her there, motionless, unable to realize what had happened to her in her medicated state. What disturbed me the most were the five different burn marks they pointed out to me. Lighter fluid was apparently used.

"The police officer who rescued her said she was trying to crawl out of a storm gutter at a traffic intersection," said Dr. Goldman. He added, "It was a miracle he didn't drive right over her. It was sheer luck that he had his windows down and heard her struggling."

"This is so unreal," I said incredulously. My entire body shook with horror. I was afraid to touch her. They, (I say they, because I couldn't imagine just one person doing this) left her for dead, in a storm gutter.

Dr. Goldman accompanied me as I gradually moved closer to her. With his guidance I was able to kiss her on the head. He showed me the best places to stroke her. And most importantly, he told me to speak calmly when I was with her. She would heal faster if she was surrounded by familiar things. Pulling off my jacket, I tucked it around her in the bed so she could smell my scent. I spoke to her for a while until she nodded off to sleep. I then left for the waiting room and sat down to recuperate.

Matt called my cell and I told him everything. He begged me to let him come down. I told him that all I would do was cry if he did, and I needed to hold it together right now. Instead, I called Carrie Warner (anorexic), my first client of the day and rescheduled her session. She obliged. I waited for the police and tried to quell my terrified feelings. The tremors in my limbs lasted for hours. The staff in the clinic each took their turn to reassure me Ginger would be fine. In the back of my mind, I knew it was true. However, in the back of my mind, I wasn't sure if *I* would make it.

# 6

# Get a Grip

I spent most of the day aimlessly walking around the animal clinic. The staff was nice enough to let me go and visit Ginger whenever I wanted. Each time I did, it became easier to see her. My tears continually rained down onto my shirt as my pain began to change into something else. Clenching and unclenching my hands, I began to pace outside in the parking lot. Every time I returned inside to visit Ginger, I saw red. I wanted blood. Who had done this? Was it the crazy mother and daughter duo?

The police arrived and I filled out a formal report. Had I left the door unlocked? Did I have any enemies? (I had to try and not laugh at that question.) The most disturbing part was the ginger root stake. Whoever had done this wanted to send a message, loud and clear. There was something I was missing. Then, I remembered the car from last night. Oh, God, the car. Even Matt had been unnerved by its presence.

"Wait, there was a car parked outside my apartment. A Chrysler. It was beige-colored and Matt said it was one of the newer models, whatever that means."

"That's good," she said jotting in her notes.

The policewoman told me they might be able to find a videotape of the event. Cameras were recording everything these days when it came to traffic intersections. Especially when the traffic light turns from yellow to red, cameras have been set up throughout the city catching drivers speeding through at the last second. Matt had been mailed a nice photo of himself several times going through a red light. It pissed him off for days at a time.

"So, you might be able to see who did it?" I asked.

"Well, yes, we might be able to see who left Ginger in the gutter. However, that might not mean it was the person who hurt her. But it might be a good lead. There are a lot of people living on the street, in and around your neighborhood. Unfortunately, sometimes they see a wounded animal and—"

"And what? They just shove the poor thing down in the city's water system? That's horrible," I said, feeling my nostrils flaring. Rage filled me to the core. And the officer took notice. She gave me a quick glance in the eye and stepped back. She decided to change the subject.

"Let's just wait until we see the video, okay?" She lightly touched my shoulder, displaying just the correct amount of affinity toward me in order to calm my rage. She promised to call me as soon as she had any information and then left the clinic.

Ginger was showing signs of movement when I went in to check on her. I forced myself to pull it together and tend to her. I stayed there for another three hours, sitting by her side, softly touching her fur. I nodded off and slept another hour until one of the nurses woke me up. They had just given Ginger a strong dose of medicine. She would sleep now for about six hours. In other words, I should go home and rest. If I had had an ounce of energy to refuse, the look in the staff's collective eyes told me they would ask me to leave, nicely of course. I wouldn't be able to help her in the shape I was in.

The rain had ceased and the pink-purple sky greeted me with its cool breeze. Driving home, I decided to call my friend Carol. I needed someone who would console me and not shove me against the fridge for a quickie. Plus, I was furious at Matt. Why didn't he insist we report that car from last night?

Carol and I had known each other since college. She was a nurse and my single female friend that I'd kept in touch with since I began dating Matt last year. She had such a sweet soul, born and raised in Oklahoma. She attended church every week and started every sentence with "Bless their heart." She also was one of the most beautiful women I'd ever met. Perfect body frame, five-foot-nine inches tall, long auburn hair, blue eyes and boobs that put every bra she wore to the test. In another life, I don't know if we would've been friends. We were like oil and water, but it worked. She answered on the third ring.

"Hey, Lins, I was just thinking about calling you!" she said, her voice full of enthusiasm.

I had to pull my car over into a gas station and park. I began sobbing out of control. Five minutes passed while my body crumpled over the steering wheel. At the same time, Carol tried to calm me down.

"Lindsey, what is it? Please tell me what happened. Is it about Matt?" she begged helplessly.

I barely managed to speak. "Ginger got outside last night and someone did atrocious things to her!"

"What? Is she okay? What happened?"

I managed to tell her the story I was sick of telling. I heard her gasp. Then she began crying herself. Some of her sobs echoed louder than my own. My entire Bluetooth-connected car reverberated with the sounds of our sadness.

A woman walked past my car. She looked all around the station to see if anyone else had noticed me. She frowned, her eyes wide. She motioned for me to roll down my window.

"God, Carol, there is a woman here. She looks worried. Hold on," I said, lowering my car window. I peered out toward her.

"Do you need help? Should I call 911?" she asked.

"No, but thank you. I just had some really bad news and I needed to pull off the road, you know?" I said.

"Okay, I wanted to make sure you're all right," she said, with a concerned look on her face.

"I'm coming over right now," Carol announced, as she had been listening.

"Okay, I'll be home in a minute," I told her.

"Bless her heart, poor Ginger," she said before hanging up.

Thankfully, I managed to get back to my apartment after hanging up with Carol. I knew she'd be the one who could put me at ease. She'd been known to be packing heat from time to time. Though she was a God-fearing woman, she loved her freedom and her men. Lots of them. In fact, the reason she kept a gun was she had almost been gang raped in a back alley one night after coming out of a bar. Although the thought of guns distressed me, somehow, the idea of having one nearby made me feel safer in the situation.

Inside my house, an eerie feeling of quiet descended upon me. My mouth was dry, and my stomach knotted into a series of pretzels. The absence of the usual feline welcome home unnerved me. I nearly called out to her once I saw her empty bowl of food.

Time to get drunk.

I reached first for the bottle of Scotch underneath the kitchen cupboard, grateful that I hadn't drunk the whole bottle during my last binge. It took seconds to down a double shot, minus the grapes. My face flushed, and a burning heat trickled down my throat, as I put my hands to my cheeks. I should have allowed Matt to come over too. My family came to mind and I almost called them. But seeing my dad's picture on the coffee table among others like mom, Carol and Matt, I couldn't go through with it. Mom had her hands full with enough right now. Dad's Alzheimer's disease had become worse over the last few months and I didn't want to add to her stress level. She had become addicted to pain pills after she broke her hip and I knew it would be a matter of time before she'd no longer be able to take care of him. Looking through all the picture frames, I picked up the one with me holding Ginger and held it to my chest.

"Lins!" The yell was accompanied by a fist hammering on the door. I went over to open it.

"Carol," I sobbed. About five minutes passed as we held each other. I was sobbing snot over her red jacket and then pathetically trying to rub it off. She kissed my hands, forehead, and the picture I was clutching of Ginger. Her affection was lovely. I'd always thought of her as both a sister and a second mother. By no fault of her own, my mother lacked giving physical affection to anyone. It wasn't her style. So Carol became a wonderful ancillary.

"I'm okay now," I said, slowly releasing myself from Carol's arms. I pretended to smile but Carol shook her head and sniggered.

"Yeah, I ain't buying that for a second." She squeezed my arm. "Now pour us another shot."

Carol stayed all night and slept on the sofa. I called the clinic several times and the nurse said Ginger was resting peacefully, but my rage still simmered under the surface. I was determined that someone would pay for what they had done.

I struggled through another restless night. Sleep decided to avoid me—mostly due to my mind conjuring up revenge scenarios, mixed with instances of pure panic and fear. It didn't help that I had to go back to work, either.

"I don't know if I can do this," I said to Carol over breakfast, which for me was just a cup of tea.

"Do what?" she asked, slurping her tea and then biting into an apple from the table.

"Everything!" Jumping up from the table, I started pacing back and forth, counting the issues on my fingers. "Deal with Ginger, go to work and listen to those people talk nonsense all day. I mean, I wanted to plan a vacation on Monday. But then I had my session with Sharon and she looked at me like I had gone off my rocker, again. So, I took on another new case for tomorrow." My voice rose to a higher octave with each word.

"Bless her heart. Do you want me to kill her off for ya?"

"Tempting, but no," I said. "And then there is Matt!"

"Matt. What did he do?" Carol asked.

"He stood me up on Monday night. I think he's lying to me about something." I could feel myself getting agitated.

"Do I have to kill him too?" Carol appeased me.

"Stop it. I know I can get paranoid sometimes. Yes, I'm insecure. But, last night there was a car parked out front. Matt seemed concerned about it at first, but then acted like it was nothing. Now my baby is recovering from someone torturing her," I said, biting my lips. I ran to the bathroom to grab a bottle of chewable antacid pills. My inflamed stomach desperately needed some relief. After downing six tablets, I returned to the kitchen table.

Carol's eyes narrowed. She offered a deep sigh of condolence. I could tell she sensed me being on the verge of another meltdown. She stood and came over to me, sitting on my lap. I squeezed her tight as she wrapped her arms around me.

"Bless your heart. I'm here for you, baby, you know that, right?" she said.

"I know." Resting my head on her shoulders, I blew her hair out of my face.

"And, I'll be more than happy to shoot off Matt's penis if you need me to." Carol chortled and I joined in with her. She had a knack of always bringing me back to reality with her sense of humor.

"I have to get in the shower and go see Ginger before my first session," I said dolefully.

"You want me to go with you? I could stay with her while you work." Her eyes lit up when she saw the relief on my face.

"You're off today?" I asked hopefully.

"Yes, ma'am, all day. Why don't you let me fix you some breakfast while you go wash up?" Carol asked.

"No, thank you, I'm not hungry," I said, waving her off.

"But you didn't eat anything last night. Wait, did you sleep okay? Maybe you should take another day off."

"No, Mother, I have to work. I'll get something for dinner tonight. Matt will come over and he usually brings something. I'm sure he has called by now." I frowned and picked up my cell, but there were no missed calls or messages. "That's odd."

"What is?" she asked.

"He never called me last night. Don't you think that's strange, with all that happened?" I said.

"Maybe, on the other hand, he might have figured you wanted some space or something? Did you say for him to come over?" Carol asked.

"No, I didn't. I did kind of brush him off when he offered his help."

"He's such a sensitive asshole," she said.

"Bless his heart!" we said in unison and laughed hysterically.

Carol provided me with a warm embrace before I dashed into the shower. My whole body ached. I didn't want to admit to Carol that I hadn't been taking care of myself at all. Basically, I'd been running on fumes as inconspicuously as I could. We drove down in our own cars to the clinic. I introduced Carol to Dr. Goldman and the staff. They all appeared to be bright and cheery.

"Ginger is doing marvelously," Dr. Goldman said.

"Thank God," I cried and hugged him.

I caught Carol's gaze from the side of the room. She performed a quick raising and lowering of her eyebrows while licking her lips. This, and the fact that her face flushed was a sure sign she was attracted to Dr. Goldman. He playfully smiled at her with a glint in his eye. And I knew in that instant, Ginger would receive the best possible medical care.

"Let me show you to Ginger's new bed," Dr. Goldman said. We followed him into an area of the clinic I hadn't been in before. It was still full of cages where animals were recovering, but it didn't have that pungent hospital aroma. They had moved her out of intensive care. Wrapped in my jacket, Ginger appeared to be comfortable. Carol placed her arms around me when she saw her. Even being a nurse hadn't prepared her for seeing what such cruelty looked like up close.

"I'm so sorry, Lindsey. I had no idea." Carol's eyes began to glisten with tears.

"It's okay," I whispered back to her. I didn't want to wake Ginger unnecessarily. But, it was too late. Her ears perked in my direction when she heard me speak. Slowly, she lifted her bandaged head and tried to meow. A modicum of a whine escaped from her mouth which exacerbated Ginger's weak state. She loved making her voice known and her current medicated condition stopped this from happening.

"Hey, my sweet baby. Mama is here now," I called out, full of relief.

She tried to move, but her body had straps holding it in place. She whined in protest. I soothed her as she watched my fingers stroke her paw. A cone placed around her neck added to her irritation.

"I know that it might not seem like it, but Ginger showing signs of anger and frustration is what we want to see. She is almost done with her pain medications. At least the stronger ones that keep her asleep," Dr. Goldman told me.

"Really? That quickly?" Carol asked.

"Yes, it appears that her burn marks were not as bad as we first suspected. We're of course watching them so they don't get infected. But second degree burns usually heal nicely. She might be able to go home by Tuesday," Dr. Goldman said, stroking Ginger conscientiously.

"I'm just so relieved," I breathed out.

Dr. Goldman opened up her kennel door and removed her IV and straps.

"That has to feel better, huh?" he asked her. Agilely scooping her up in his arms, he then carried her past me. A nurse motioned for me to follow him and I sat down in the chair as he lifted her up and placed her on a table with soft guarded rails.

"She's still a bit edgy and doesn't understand what happened, so it's good that you spend some time with her, like this," he said.

"Okay, I will." And I took my turn as nurse while Carol asked questions to keep Dr. Goldman's attention. I simply shook my head and laughed. The woman had no shame.

I spent a good hour attending to Ginger and then turned over the task to Carol. No time for dawdling as Carrie Warner might have already arrived at my office. I drove with purpose, mastering the art of weaving in and around drivers who were slow moving. It wasn't until I pulled up in front of my office that I saw it. A beige Chrysler parked in front of my building. I studied it for a while before opening my side door. No one was inside it, so I walked over and snapped a few pictures of the license plate and car with my cell phone.

## 7

# Pushing Buttons

Carrie Warner jumped out of her skin when I entered the waiting room. Dressed from head to toe in white, she let out a gasp and her hands clenched into fists.

"I'm sorry, I'm sorry. I didn't mean to scare you," I said, holding out my hands.

"I thought you were already in your office," she said breathlessly pointing at the door.

"Breathe, it's okay, calm down. Just wait here a few minutes, I'll be right with you." Waving my hands to make her serene, I had to get in my office and call Matt about the car.

Once the lights were on and I threw my personal belongings in the locked cabinet, I flicked through the photos of the beige car on my cell phone. Without warning, it rang, causing me to jump in surprise. The phone slipped out of my fingers and bounced a couple of times on the floor. The final bouncing sound was not a pleasant one. Something had shattered.

"Shit!" Bending down to pick it up, my hands were shaking. "Hello?"

"Hi, sweetheart, how are you? How's Ginger?" Matt said.

"Matt, oh my God, I think the person who hurt Ginger is parked outside my building right now." Tears plummeted down my face.

"What did you say?" he asked. "Lindsey...I can't..." With a loud crackle, his voice disappeared.

"Matt? Can you hear me?" I said. Hissing sounds filled my ear. Then the phone went dead.

"Fuck! Goddammit!" I kept trying to press the buttons on the cell phone but the screen stayed black. I rushed to the window that faced the front end of the parking lot. Peeking out through the shades, I tried not to be seen from the street. Whoever owned the beige Chrysler could be looking in my direction—stalking me. The parking space where the car had been was empty. I delicately cleared a path through the shades with my fingers. I peered out, then, closed them again. I exhaled, realizing this entire time I'd forgotten to breathe.

"Carrie," I yelled, opening the door into the waiting room. "I'll be back in a jiffy, okay?" I managed to startle her again.

"Jesus," she replied, snapping her head up, showing me those awful teeth.

Going back to my desk, I used the office phone to call Matt. I assured him I was fine, and told him about my phone. He said the photos I'd taken of the car could be retrieved whether the phone was broken or not. I called security, just to be on the safe side. Ben, Mr. Orange, (my sobriquet) answered.

"Hi, Ben?" I said, trying not to sound crazy.

"Yes, Ms. CarMichael, what can I do for you?"

"Nothing, I mean. It's ridiculous. I'm being paranoid about this, but my cat was attacked a couple of days ago and—"

"I'm so sorry," he apologized, interrupting me.

"Thank you," I said, holding back the floodgates that were rapidly approaching. "The thing is," I continued, "there was a car parked outside my apartment which tore off once I noticed it. Then later that night my cat was attacked."

"So, you think you're in danger?"

"Well, I could be. I saw the car just now when I came to work. It was parked just outside. I went over and snapped a few photos of it on my cell phone. But being so jumpy when I got to my office, I dropped it. I can't get it to work anymore." I collapsed on my sofa.

"Get your phone over to the police and tell me about the car." Ben spoke in an authoritative tone, which eased my jumpy nerves. I told him what the car looked like. He said he'd pass the word on to everyone there. I went to use my bathroom and tried to compose myself. Being jittery in front of a client was never appropriate. I smoothed out my skirt and adjusted my purple sweater while looking at myself in the mirror. I brushed my hair to cover my face as much as I could; the dark circles under my eyes and pale skin proved that the last few days had done a number on me. I took a deep breath. It was time to take on Carrie Warner.

~⌐

"I'm ready for you now," I said, slowly opening the door. "No more surprises, I promise."

Carrie conspicuously raised her head and I had to force myself not to gag. She had been wiggling her top tooth. The fluid motion of her fingers and her blank stare sickened me. I glanced down and saw in her other hand she had a tooth in her palm, the bloody root edge still visible.

"It's okay," she said, laughing. "I do this all the time. My teeth are pretty loose."

"Come in and sit down," I instructed. This day had taken on a whole new level of bizarreness.

"Yes, sir," she said with a sarcastic salute.

She passed by me forcefully. I took a step backward as she invaded my personal space. Never once had I backed away before. But then, never before had my cat been tortured. *Did she own the beige Chrysler?* I shook my head. If she did, then how was it no longer parked outside, while she was in my waiting room? Following behind her toward my desk, she flicked her head around and smiled at me, causing me to stop. I could have sworn she made a hissing sound. Was I going crazy?

"Sorry, I didn't mean to surprise you," she said. Carrie began humming and ignored me while she settled on the sofa. I shook off my irrational thoughts and guessed that she was just trying to get back at me for scaring her in the waiting room. Either that, or she had taken drugs. I couldn't tell with her eyes being as large as they were.

"You seem to be enjoying yourself." I moved robotically to sit at my desk. *Should I call the police?*

"What do you mean?" she asked, sticking her tongue out at me.

"Are you on any drugs, Carrie?" I cleared my throat, adjusting the sweater around my neck.

Carrie's smile widened and she started laughing. She grabbed a pillow and pressed her face into it, but despite the attempts to muffle her laughter, she couldn't seem to stop her sudden hysterical giggles.

"Did you bring the journal I asked you to keep?" I interrupted her. Something had definitely snapped inside her mind.

"Huh?" Carrie paused in her giggles to stare at me.

"I'm sorry I had to make you wait so long to start your session, Carrie, but right now, you are acting inappropriately."

"I was just laughing. Why is that inappropriate?" she asked with a grin, ready to set off again.

"You were yanking out your teeth in my waiting room and then laughing as if you were a child," I said. Carrie pulled up the pillow to her face once more. This time, a loud toe-curling scream escaped her mouth. Then she smothered her mouth again with the pillow. "Carrie!" I half-stood, wondering if I should go reach for the panic button under my desk.

She saw my gesture and rapidly shook her head. "I'll stop. I'll stop. Please don't press the button," she begged. Regaining her composure, Carrie sat up straight.

"Show me your journal, please," I asked, realizing what was making her act this way.

"I didn't bring it, sorry," she said, jutting her chin out in defiance.

"You're high from starving yourself, aren't you?" I cocked my head to the side and pursed my lips.

"I don't get high," she said, raising her eyebrows. The sneer surfaced again. Apparently, I had hit the nail on the head. Time to see how far I could go. Time to push her buttons.

"Yes, it's like I told you earlier this week. When you starve yourself, you deny your brain nutrition too. Hence, your laughing fits," I said, maintaining eye contact.

"If you say so." Carrie looked away and lowered her chin to her chest. Her posture sagged.

"I do say so. This is basic science. You can look it up anywhere. Your issues are about power and control—not food. You like being in control, don't you?"

Carrie's eyes darted from side to side. Her mouth stiffened, then she began twitching, biting her lower lip with her top teeth. She ran her left hand up and down the side of her body. Her bony fingers began to dance with inaudible sound. She slipped one hand underneath her shirt, moving it up to her breast.

"What are you doing?" I leaned back.

"Touching myself?" Carrie licked her lips.

"Let's see how much you weigh," I said, charging at her. She resisted for show. Her arm went limp in my hand. I dragged her like one of those stuffed animals she'd played with earlier in the week. Carrie tumbled to her knees.

"Get up!" I waited a second before I pulled her up. As we stood face to face, I saw her eyes bulging out of her head, mouth opened, ready to scream. "In this room, I'm the one in control," I said.

"Please, I don't want to go in there," she cried.

Ignoring her petition, I opened the bathroom door, violently slamming it against the opposite wall. The crashing sound made her cover her ears. I shoved Carrie inside and forced her to step on the scale. *This isn't me. I'm not supposed to treat patients like this. Never!*

"Step on the scale," I commanded, pulling at her shoulders in order to get her in place. Her body stood still. I could see Carrie holding her breath in the mirror's reflection. Her eyes closed tightly. The scale confirmed my suspicion. She weighed eighty-nine pounds. "Open your eyes," I said in a controlled whisper. "Open them!"

Carrie moved as I asked, and clear droplets of tears bounced to the floor. She glanced at the scale. Seeing what she weighed, she showed a slight grin. When she caught me looking at her in the mirror, she ceased.

"No use trying to hide it." I placed my hands on my hips. "You're happy, I can tell." My eyes narrowed at her.

"Why can't I be happy? Why won't you just let me be? I'm so tired of all this shit!" Carrie screamed through her tears.

"This is why," I said and shoved her off the scale—positioning her in front of the full-length mirror. Smashing her face so she couldn't move, I used both my hands to rest her forehead upward. Carrie let out a squeal. I restrained her entire body against the mirror.

"You're hurting me," she cried as she pathetically tried to pull back.

"You are the one hurting yourself. I'm not letting go until you look in the mirror for five minutes."

"No, I won't, you crazy bitch. Let me go!" she said vehemently.

I waited for her to scratch me or punch me—anything. She had access to her arms and legs. She could have physically fought me. But, she didn't. Someone had restrained her before. It was not new to her.

"Open your eyes."

"NO!"

"Open your eyes right now or I'm admitting you back into the hospital," I said balefully.

The emotional baggage was released as Carrie slowly opened the lids of her eyes. She began sobbing uncontrollably. I eased up on my grip. Her body started shaking when she released each breath. Her mouth parted. I could tell she was struggling to speak, find the right words.

"Good, now step back and look at your body up and down." This would be a major achievement if I could manage to pull this off.

Carrie lifted her head up to the mirror and became docile. She glared at her face first. She had inflamed eyes, extended bones from her cheeks and jaw. She touched her face, chin. Maybe this had been the first time in months? The first time she'd really seen what her body looked like.

"What do you feel right now?" I asked.

"I feel ugly," she said in a monotone voice.

"Why?"

"Because," she commenced with the tears, "I allowed them to make me want to be this way." Carrie clutched her arms around her stomach.

"Who?" I held my breath.

"Those boys at the party I was at in high school. They got me drunk and took me to a bedroom. Three of them took their turns raping me. I screamed for help, begging them to stop. But they just kept on going." Carrie turned quickly and hugged me.

Painstakingly, the source of all her angst had been revealed.

"I'm so sorry," I said, trying to soothe her. "They have no control over you anymore." This made Carrie break down further. I held her tightly as her knees buckled. After a few minutes of this, Carrie looked at me. She was calm, serene even. She no longer had to keep the horrendous secret to herself.

"That was a big step for you," I said, lifting her chin.

"I know," she nodded, "Is it okay if I use the sink to wash my face?"

"Of course," I agreed. As I went to leave her, I caught a glance of my own appearance in the mirror. I was shocked by what I saw, dirty hair, dark circles under my eyes, with an ashen complexion. I couldn't tell which one of us looked worse. All I needed to do was lose about twenty pounds and then we'd be twins.

Once Carrie returned to my office, I saw lightness in her step. She smiled.

"Can I ask why you are smiling?" I watched her move across the room.

"Oh, it's nothing really. It's not even funny, but, this is why my marriage failed. My husband thought I was ugly."

"He didn't say that, did he?" I shook my head.

"He didn't have to say it. I could tell he hated to look at me. He stopped being affectionate. His words even sounded cold. Then he stopped wanting to have sex with me. So, I started starving myself even more," Carrie said, wiping her nose with a tissue. "I wanted him to see me starve. It was my way to get back at him. Six months later, he left for work one day and said he wanted a divorce as he walked out."

"What did you say?"

"Nothing, I went to the bathroom and stuck my finger down my throat. Out flew my breakfast. He admitted to me when he came home that night, he had been seeing another woman. Truth be told, I expected it." Carrie shrugged half-heartedly.

"Did you ever tell anyone about the rape?" I asked, changing the subject. She'd never recover if we didn't deal with this issue first.

Carrie paused. "I told my mother. She grounded me for a week and said I deserved it, for going to the party without permission and dressing the way I did."

"She was wrong." I felt my whole body tighten.

"I know that now, but at the time it happened I was a virgin. I knew nothing about sex. Mom was a devout Catholic and I got pregnant." Every word that came out of Carrie's mouth was matter-of-fact. She showed no emotional attachment to the entire event.

"What happened then? What about your father?"

"Dad was never in my life. He left when Mom got pregnant with me. She got a job as a nurse and homeschooled me until I went to college. I had a little girl." Carrie hesitated. "She was placed up for adoption. I never even held her. They told me I could, but, I knew she wasn't mine anymore." Carrie stared blankly. She lifted her hands, palms up.

"There is a lot here to digest. First, allow me to say I'm very sorry that all this happened to you."

"Thank you."

"Would you like to tell the police about the rape?"

"God, no. I want it all behind me."

Leaning in toward Carrie, I said, "I think you're within the statute of limitations. Wouldn't you like to have justice for all the years you spent in pain?"

"I have no case. I watch TV, you know."

"Then, you must also realize that confronting someone who raped you, even if you lose the case, will make you feel better?" I knew she'd say no, but I had to push a tiny bit so she wouldn't regret it later. "Will you at least think about it?" I tilted my head upward.

"I'll think about it. No promises, okay?" she nodded.

"Okay." A moment of silence passed. "Why did you lose your job as a teacher?" The subject needed to be changed. I didn't want her to backtrack to the baby. It had to be left for another session.

"I was taking too many sick days when I started not eating. One of the other teachers caught me in the bathroom sticking my finger down my throat. It was something I did early on until I devised a plan of avoiding people's attention. That's also when my marriage fell apart and I gave up caring if someone caught me. So, I moved home with good old Mom. End of story." She laughed.

"No," I told her. "It's just the beginning."

We both exchanged a smile.

"The funny part is, all I *really* want to do now is have sex," she said.

"Why would that be funny? That's actually a good, healthy sign. You should celebrate it," I said triumphantly.

"Celebrate?" Her tone was ambiguous.

"Sexual desire is life-affirming, it means you want to connect again," I said, raising my arms up in the air.

"I'm not doing one of those online dating services if that's what you're getting at!" Carrie snickered.

Carrie and I had a good close to the session. Since I had missed one of her days this past week, I had to see her again tomorrow. We scheduled the time for 1:00 p.m.

# 8

# Lunch Break

I went to the window and watched Carrie leave the building. There was still no sign of the beige Chrysler. I checked my watch, ninety minutes until my next session. I grabbed my broken cell phone and decided to go over to the police station. Although every part of my body was against me doing it, in case I'd run into certain people from the past.

Ben greeted me in the hallway at his usual desk. Downing a sandwich, his feet up on the edge watching his monitor, he coughed when he saw me approach. Then he placed down his wrapper. *Oh, yeah, food, lunch.* Sunlight gleamed through the glass windows. I averted my eyes.

"I'm stepping out for a while, Ben," I said, searching through my purse for sunglasses.

"You going to the police station?" Ben looked seriously at me while sipping his soda.

"Yep, then I'll stop by the vet clinic and see how Ginger is doing."

Ben stood wiping his hands with a napkin. The sun's reflection bounced off his rubious hair. Straightening his shoulders and pushing out his chest, God, he looked desirable. The tension going up and down my spine ceased. He had a calming effect on me.

"That's good. Give her a hug from me, okay? I told everyone on duty to be on the lookout for the car. And they were all real upset to hear what happened to you. So, please know, we've got your back." Ben's chin quivered.

"Thank you." I looked down, afraid I would start crying again.

He moved toward the glass door and opened it for me.

"I'll hold down the fort till you get back," he said. Walking past him, I could smell his sweet orange scented aftershave mixed with pastrami. His slight beard stubble was showing. It might have been cool outside, but there was a definite exchange of body heat between us. I wanted to taste his lips.

"I'm counting on you," I said, flitting my eyes. This would be the highlight of my day. Spending a tender second alone with a police officer who'd never judged me on my past even when it was apparent some of his friends had. When I started working here, there had been the usual rumors and whispers about me. But not a word came from Ben, he was first class all the way. He made sure the other ones—who enjoyed laughing at me under their breath when I had passed by in the hall—stopped at once. Nothing got past him.

Milo Cooper was at 2:00 p.m. Then, the new patient—what the fuck was his name?—at 4:00 p.m.

I parked my car at the police station. This place brought back a flood of memories. Ones that I thought I had under control, but I was fooling myself. Instead, I stared at the flat, one-story building that snaked around the whole street. I wanted to call Matt, but my phone was shattered. We might have been going through a rough patch, but he stood by me when he learned the truth about me last year. Many men would have jumped ship. But he didn't. Sometimes I wish he had. The look in his eyes wasn't the same endearing one after I told him. Instead of holding me up on a pedestal like he used to, now I was just a broken piece of furniture that he'd gotten from the flea market.

"Okay, you *can* do this," I said, whispering to myself as I rubbed my hands down my pants. I hated when my hands sweat. As I got out of the car, I had a déjà vu feeling and it wasn't a pleasant one. The inhabitants of the gravelly structure made me feel uneasy. It crept over me, forcing me to check all the doors that led into the building and exited back. I wallowed on the sidewalk and saw leaves flying across the pavement. Two separate pairs of cops walked by me as I entered. Using my hands to cover my face every chance I could, I tentatively approached the front desk.

A black man greeted me behind a huge counter, tapping his pencil on a clipboard. The whole area was neatly organized. His eyes darted back and forth toward me and his computer screen. He took several breaths and rested his chin on his hand. "Can I help you?" he said, pursing his lips.

"Yes, I have an open case number," I told him with a shaky voice.

He stared at me with a blank face. For a split second, I panicked. I was ready to bolt. He raised his eyebrows and held out his hand.

"Do you have a card or the case number handy?" he asked.

"Oh, yes, right here." Rummaging through my purse, I found the police card that the female officer handed me earlier. "Here it is." I handed it to him with a huge sigh of relief.

He looked me over for a second and then he typed in the numbers. While waiting for my story to appear on screen, he tapped his fingers on the desk as if there was music playing. He shook his head.

"Sorry this is taking so long," he said.

"It's all right," I replied, pulling my hair over my face. *Please don't remember me, I remember you from that night.*

"Here it is." He paused as he took a breather to read over the record. I began scratching my hands and felt dizzy.

"Oh, I am sorry. How is your cat doing?" he asked in a soothing tone.

"She is much better, thank you. The doctor expects a full recovery except for her eye, of course," I said quickly. The longer this took, the more anxious I became.

"Aw, that's terrible." He rolled his head downward.

With his sympathetic words and gestures, I began to feel more at ease. I wasn't afraid to tell him the rest.

"I need to speak to whoever is assigned to my case. Because the car that was stalking my house the night Ginger was hurt—I don't know if it's the same one or not, but I think I saw it parked in the business complex where I work."

The officer again raised his eyebrows.

"In fact, the car was parked there today." I reached for the broken cell phone. "I took a few photos of it on my phone, including the license plate," I said.

"Good, that's great," he said with his eyes all aglow.

"But, then I dropped it on the floor and I think it's broken now." I frowned.

The officer signaled for me to give him the phone. I did.

"Hey, Ted!" he yelled, turning his back toward me.

"Yeah! What ya need?" Another male voice came from the back.

Ted examined me around the corner with his blue eyes. Bending down to tie his shoe laces, dressed in jeans and a brown shirt. He grabbed my phone and looked up at me with a sorrowful glance.

"Well, this doesn't look like it will work, does it?" Ted said with a smirk.

"I know." I faked a smile.

"Let me see if I can do a little magic with it, okay?" Ted said.

"Yes, please do whatever you can. Thank you!"

"Ted, we need the photos of a license plate. Here is the case number," the officer added. He wrote everything down for Ted. Then Ted disappeared as fast as he entered.

"If he can't fix it nobody can. Do you need anything else?"

"No, you have all my info. Just have someone contact me when they know anything, please," I said, and turned to leave. My knees shook. I shouldn't have come here without Matt.

"Ms. CarMichael?" The officer stopped me. "We have your home and work phone number, correct?" He turned the screen around for me to verify everything. I gaped. Composing myself, I went over to check the monitor. The officer's eyes peered at me. I was getting uncomfortable.

"Yes, this is all correct." I spoke quickly.

"CarMichael? That name sounds familiar. Have I met you before?" he said, wrinkling his brow.

"No, I don't think so," my voice quivered.

"We'll give you a call as soon as we can," he said, eyeing me firmly.

"Thanks." I pivoted around and tried to look casual as I exited.

I blasted out to the parking lot. Finding refuge in the safety of my car, I locked the doors and tried to imagine none of this was real. Placing my hands on my cheeks, I calmed myself. The hardest part was not having my cell phone. I had no one to call. What would have happened if I had a full-fledged anxiety attack? I shook those thoughts out of my head and thought of Ginger. She needed me. She survived a brutal experience. I could manage my day with the knowledge she was coming home soon. Simple as that.

Soon I was back in my office complex. I couldn't recall how I'd driven back. People and cars had been a blur. No beige Chrysler of any model was parked in the vicinity.

Inside the building, Ben waved hello while talking on the phone. Good thing he had been distracted as my communication skills were not up to par. I waved back while walking to my office. "Get yourself together Lindsey, you're a therapist," I sobbed as soon as I closed my door. My body leaned against the wall for support. The phone rang.

"Hello?"

"Lins? How are you?" Matt asked.

"I survived the police station if that's what you're asking." Tears streamed down my chin.

"Oh, baby, I should have done that for you."

"No, it's okay. I'm all right." I settled myself down. "You want to come over later?"

"Yeah, I'll bring some dinner too."

"Thanks, sweetie," I said pulling at my hair, then curled up on my couch. My droopy eyes wanted a nap. My lids were heavy and I obliged. Just for a few minutes' sleep.

The office phone forced me to wake. I reached over to grab it, half asleep.

"Lindsey? Is that you?" my mother asked.

"Mom, yeah. It's me, how are you?"

"Oh honey, your father has taken a spell for the worse. We had to admit him to that nursing home at Coral Bay."

I rolled up, no longer dazed. "We, who do you mean, we?"

"Maggie from next door helped me." Mom's words were full of sobs. "I went shopping and when I returned home, your dad had disappeared. I got hysterical and banged on Maggie's door for help. We looked for him for three hours."

"Why didn't you call me?" I hollered.

"I did, but your phone said it was out of service. Don't scream at me! I was terrified. We found him going through a dumpster in a back alley down the street. Someone had called the police on him. Oh, Lins! He had jumped inside all that trash."

"It's okay now. Mom, calm down. He's in a safe place." I allowed her to spew her burdens on me and never said a word about my own. That was how our relationship worked. I learned early on that Mom's needs were far more important than mine, even when I was a child.

"How will I ever live without him?" she begged me to answer.

"You'll visit him every day," I said. "It won't be easy at first, but it will get better. We both knew this day was coming, right?" I felt a lump in my throat.

"Do you promise? You promise it will get better?" Mom asked quickly. I hated that question. I despised her tone, not the weakness of it, but the sound I grew to know when she had taken her pain medication. She was high. I thought it selfish of her.

Dad had always been the stronger one, a district attorney for Palm Beach County. Now he was disappearing before our very eyes. The knotting muscles inside my legs kept my feet frozen. I began to panic again. All I wanted at the beginning of the week had been some vacation time. When I asked, the answer was no. I accepted that. But, now, all *this* had happened. I was going to give Sharon a piece of my mind as soon as I saw her.

"Listen, Mom, I have a two o'clock session that I need to keep. Then, I will cancel the rest of them and meet you tonight at Coral Bay Nursing Home. I promise. Okay? If you need to get a hold of me, call me at work or home. My cell phone is broken."

"Come as soon as you can." Mom sounded desperate.

"I will, I have had a really bad week and rescheduled my patients to begin with, Mom. Please understand. Dad and you will be okay until this evening. Just try to be calm. It will be all right."

"All right," she cried, "take care of yourself." Mom acknowledged my existing life.

"You too, bye, Mom." Taking deep breaths, I stared at the wall, not hanging the phone up. I didn't think I could take anyone else calling. The room started to close in on me. *How was Ginger?* I tossed my patient list with names and numbers on the desk. Connecting the phone, I made the calls.

I rescheduled Carrie for Monday. She was thrilled.

I rescheduled the new patient, Kevin Marshal and family; they weren't.

I just had Milo Cooper's session to make it through. I needed a raise.

# 9

# Milo Cooper

Thursday January 9th, 2014, Thirty-eighth
Session 2:00p.m.

The green light blinked. Milo was 'in the house' as he loved to say. He also loved giving in to his wife's every whim. I adjusted my sweater so that my breasts were not easily apparent. He had a knack for staring. Gazing in the mirror, I adjusted my ponytail in back. I looked and felt like shit. This session had to be a short one.

"Hi, Milo, come on in," I welcomed him through the doorway.

"Hello," he said in his usual deep tone. He didn't even blink an eye at my appearance. A woman was to be treated like gold no matter how much she let herself go. And, yes, he still took a gander at my boobs while he walked inside. He hastily averted his eyes as he knew I'd asked him several times not to stare at me. He was always apologetic but he never changed his actions. One of the many issues we had been working on, still.

"Take a seat, tell me what's going on," I said with narrowed lips.

"Ah, where to begin?" Milo said, while sprawling his arms over the back of the sofa. He crossed his eyes and smirked.

"Something funny?" I inquired.

Milo straightened out his expression and leaned his elbows over both legs. "Not funny, no, just the usual stuff."

He apparently didn't receive the memo. I had major life issues to contend with today. I wasn't in the mood for his sickening-poor relationship skills, or what he thought of as his witty sense of humor.

"And what's the usual stuff?" I attempted to keep him focused as my tolerance for bullshit was at zero. "How are things with your wife going?" I clicked my pen off and on near my head, not yet looking at him.

Milo dived into another fit of snickers. "Just grand," he said with an Irish accent. "I can't tell, if she hates me, or merely despises me this week. There is just such a subtle difference between the two of those feelings, I no longer can tell." He chortled.

"Did she say she hates you?" I asked, turning toward him.

"Yes, I know, it's not funny. But sometimes I need to laugh or else I think I might go crazy." Milo began to squirm on the sofa.

*Oh, wonderful,* I thought, *he's having some major problems that I can't sweep under the rug until next week.*

"Here I am, living with a woman I promised to love and cherish for the rest of my life and she tells me she hates me at least once a day. It's pathetic." Milo lowered his chin to his chest, shutting his eyes.

"And why do you stay with her if she says that?" I already knew, but wanted to have him say it out loud.

"Because I think I deserve to be treated like the loser I am."

"A loser, huh? So, if you're a loser, that means you don't deserve to be respected or loved, right?" I asked.

"Yes, I know it's wrong. But I'm not ready to give up on our marriage yet." Milo's mouth twitched. He leaned back in his seat.

"Does your wife still refuse to attend any sessions with you?" I asked.

"Oh, no, are you kidding?" He looked to the ceiling. "In fact, the more I come here, the more she's convinced I'm the one with all the problems. I'm the one who is destroying our marriage," he said.

"Wait, I don't understand. Does your wife think that I tell you that in order for your marriage to work, you, not she, has to be in therapy?" I pondered.

"Of course," he shrugged.

"It's not true! Don't you see how she's manipulating you?"

"You've lost me." Milo rubbed his hands through his hair.

"First, she tells you therapy might be a good idea for you. Then, when you prove her right and keep coming here, it's still not good enough, so?" I widen my eyes to see if Milo caught my drift.

Unfortunately, he shook his head. His eyes went blank.

"Let me say this as plainly as possible. As long as your wife refuses to attend therapy, whether it's marriage counseling or individual sessions, the problem will stay the same." I sat back and looked at him firmly.

"I guess, but I am the man after all. I should be able to make my wife happy. I should learn how to become a better husband." His voice sounded defensive. I rolled my eyes.

"Yes, but a marriage involves two people. Not just someone who decides the other person should learn to be a better husband. Why don't you suggest she learn to become a better wife? If she is truly committed to the marriage, shouldn't she want to be involved in the process of making it better?"

Milo shifted his body movement again. He said nothing.

"Let me ask a different kind of question, Milo. How would you feel if the roles were reversed? If you refused to work on your marriage until she sought individual therapy?" I raised my eyebrows.

"Are you kidding me? She'd never go for it and she'd send me packing with divorce papers. Don't get me wrong, I'd fucking love it if she would agree. But, the woman simply believes that her shit doesn't stink. Yeah, I come from a fucked up family, I'll admit it. But at least I'm willing to work on my issues. I've never cheated on her. I've never told her all the things I don't like about her. And, I've never once hit her, even when she pounds on me." Milo's eyes gazed downward.

"Is she *still* hitting you?" I waved my hand to stop him. "You know we've discussed this. Milo, you can call the police, right?

There is no shame in being abused by a woman." I straightened my shoulders.

Milo's face turned a lovely hue of pink. He pursed his lips then lowered his head once more and nodded.

"I know. I just don't think of it at the time it's happening. By the time she's hitting me, I just try to protect myself. She has this point of no return and once she crosses over, I wait it out."

"No, no fight that causes violent behavior is an ordinary fight." I shook my head. "It's never okay to hit anyone, not a woman, not a man or a child. Don't forget you can call the police and press charges on her. Then, she would have to get therapy. It will get worse, Milo. I know from experience."

Milo's face went blank.

"Can you tell me what happened?"

"I'd rather not. If that's okay for now."

We stayed silent as I could see the expression on his face. He was embarrassed, not meeting my eyes. Whether or not he got the message I had given would take time. Time he didn't have.

"How are things at work going?" I needed to change the subject. His ego had been trampled on enough.

"I can't get a manager's job to save my ass. My old boss, that horrible bitch, burned my record." Milo looked at me while cracking his knuckles.

"Why not just take what's available?"

"Because, it's the best way to get the highest salary," he said, running his hand through his straw-colored hair.

"So, you're not open to any other type of work other than fast-food service?" I opened my palms toward him.

Milo provided me a look of exasperation. "I can't, it's all I know how to do! I can't go back to school, because I have no money. I won't be approved for a student loan, because my credit sucks. I'm trapped! Everywhere I look, I'm trapped! My own wife hates me, people at work hate me. Hell, even I wouldn't be friends with me if I met myself walking down the street!" he growled.

This time, it was me who pushed back in my seat. His violent tone switched on a rush of adrenalin inside me. I didn't physically fear him, but, when dealing with a person who had a fragile ego, it was best not to push my luck. After a pause of silence between us, I broke the tension.

"Let's get back to basics, shall we?" I said steadily.

"What do you mean?"

"Why did you seek out therapy to begin with?"

I saw it in his body language, his posture straightening, and hands gripped together tightly.

"My wife thought I needed help. She thought I wasn't acting normal for my age. She and I were arguing all the time. Then one night she hit me several times. I was never the same after that. I'm afraid to argue with her," he breathed out.

"And even though she was violent toward you, you chose to stay?"

"Yes."

"You attended thirty-eight sessions all by yourself."

"Yes."

"Even though she was the one who hit you? Even though she's the one who still berates your actions and makes lists of what you do wrong?"

"I get the feeling you're trying to tell me something," he said, averting his eyes.

"Yes," I said.

"I'm just going through the motions of what I'm supposed to do here. To be honest, I think I am a sex addict."

"Why do you think that? Did your wife say you were?"

"Yes, I watch porn on my computer and sometimes even on my BlackBerry while sitting in the living room alone. That's sick, isn't it?"

"I thought you said you have never cheated on your wife?"

"I haven't."

"Then, I think you're confusing being a sex addict with just being a guy." I smiled. "In order to be addicted to sex, one engages in sexual acts with many different people. I assume that's not what you're doing."

"God! No. But, why do I still feel guilty?"

"Do you ever watch porn sitting next to your wife?" I asked.

"No. She'd kill me right then and there," he said as his eyes widened.

"Have you watched porn on your BlackBerry at other places?"

"Sure, the mall, where we shop and sometimes at work if it's a slow day," he laughed.

"Has anyone ever caught you watching porn?" I asked.

"Yeah, but I just tell them I'm watching the financial markets, even though I don't have a penny to my name." Milo slapped his knee as if he had just presented the greatest faux pas in history.

"Milo, it's not funny. And, yes, it does sound that your fascination with pornography will need to be addressed. We don't want this to become an issue that further divides you and your wife. I've known you for quite a while now and you never said anything about watching porn incessantly," I said sternly.

"Oh, really?"

"Yes."

"But it would be okay for me to watch porn as long as I don't cheat on my wife. Not to sound graphic, but all I do is jerk off. My dad said it's okay. He told me my mom knew he watched porn all the time and she didn't care."

"I'm not sure I agree with him. I think this might cause a whole bunch of problems if your wife found out. She is already looking for a way to be angry with you. So, I'm concerned." I leaned down and rested my arms on my knees.

"Do you think it's that bad? I do it out of sheer boredom most of the time." Milo took exception to my comments.

"I'm afraid you're going to end up deliberately destroying your marriage."

"NO!" His anger was surfacing.

"Milo, be honest with yourself. You've been down this road before," I pushed.

Milo jumped out of his seat. This time his face turned purple.

I stood up too, in reaction.

"I won't sabotage my marriage. I have it under control. I just wish all the women in my life would give me a break. I am a nice guy."

"Milo, calm down. Breathe slowly, okay? I believe you are a very nice guy."

He paced back and forth in the room. "Then what's wrong with me? Why is every fucking day a struggle? Why do I hate driving home to my own house?"

"I think you're stuck in the mud. Until you discover your self-worth and learn self-respect you're going to stay stuck," I said.

"Okay, okay, I get it," he said, violently shaking his head. "God, what you must think of me. I am pathetic. I never should have gotten married. I wasn't ready and she forced me into it. Like everything else, either I marry her or she'd break up with me." He paused. "I should have run like hell in the opposite direction," Milo snickered.

"Milo, look at me." I nimbly touched his arm. His gaze fixed on mine. Tears had begun to form. "I believe in you. Okay? I believe you are a wonderful person who got sucked into a bad relationship." And I did believe in him. He would be a great catch for the right woman. First, he had a decent amount of work to do on himself. "Sit back down."

He returned to the couch and the floodgates opened. After a good few rounds of sobbing, I focused his attention back on me.

"We need to set some goals for you, now, as it appears you've reached a plateau in our sessions and you are not just hanging around there, you're backsliding."

"Yeah, yep," he sniffled.

"Now think of something you can choose for a new goal. Something that's doable, not unrealistic."

"Honestly, I have no idea. I just want to be happy, that's all," he said reluctantly.

"I think we need to hit this head on," I told him.

"How?"

"I want to have another session with you on Monday," I paused, bracing myself. "And I want you to think about if you really want to stay married to your wife." I waited for the blow-up reaction, but it never came. Milo stared, that's all.

"Is this one of those questions, like, where do I see myself in five years? You know the kind they ask you on job interviews?"

"Yes, it's exactly like that. Life is so short, Milo. Why live the short amount of time you have being unhappy?"

"What if I bring this up to her and she kicks me out and I have nowhere to live?" he asked, breathing quickly.

I shrugged my shoulders. "That *is* a possibility. But, deep down inside I think you've always known that was a possibility. She has been blackmailing you for years with it. But I fear her words and actions toward you are more damaging than you let yourself believe. Maybe some time away from her would be a good thing? Do you have any friends or family you could stay with if you needed to?"

"Yeah, I have a friend who knows I'm unhappy. He knows I've been seeing you too. Can I call him now?" Milo asked while retrieving his phone from his pocket.

"Go ahead," I said.

Milo had a rough time telling his friend the truth. He broke down several times, but in the end, he said he'd let him live with him if it came to that.

Distracted and exhausted, I scheduled Milo's appointment for 1:00 p.m. on Monday. It was the same time I had set up for Carrie Warner and I didn't realize it at that point.

Milo's session passed its usual time. So, I checked on how Ginger was doing by calling Carol.

"I think I'm in love," Carol announced.

"Boy, that was fast. You're sure you've never met before?" I teased. *Bless his heart.*

"Oh, Ginger is doing great!" she added.

"Really? That's the best news I've had all day." I began to tear up.

"The doctor and I have been flirting non-stop," she giggled. I wiped my nose with a tissue. Carol realized something had upset me.

"Are you crying?" she paused.

"No, well, a little," I admitted. "Mom called me and she said my dad got lost and was found in a trash dumpster. So, she had to take him to stay at the Coral Bay Nursing Home."

"Bless your heart! Here I am laughing about my love life and you have all this going on! Why didn't you stop me?"

"To tell you the truth, I just enjoyed listening to something normal for a little while," I laughed, blowing my nose.

"Oh, sweetie. I'm so sorry."

"Thanks, I'm on my way home now to pack some things and I'll be heading over there soon. Mom sounded frantic of course, she has no clue what's been going on with me."

"Is she still taking all that Vicodin?"

"Yep, she was high as a kite when I spoke to her." I felt my pulse rise. "I have to go. I'll talk to you soon, okay?"

"Sure, honey, bye."

My stomach growled and my mouth had started to grow a cactus from lack of food and water. I washed up in the bathroom, applied as much concealer as humanly possible, and went out to get some coffee in the cafeteria next door.

Ben wasn't at his desk. In fact, no one was there at all. I found them all sitting together with trays full of hamburgers and sodas— laughing it up at a table. *God, I wanted to sit with them*, I thought. Every inch of my body ached. They all waved at me when I walked in the room. I told them I was running late and couldn't stop to chat. A unified moan came from their table in the brightly lit room. I moaned too, making fun of them.

Secretly, I knew the person who really wanted me to sit with them was Ben. They all had managed to disguise their uneasy feelings about me, but it was still there—hiding just below the surface. I saw it in the way they turned their heads, glancing down or nodding to each other. The way they whispered or clammed up when I entered the room. Or, maybe I had become paranoid. I didn't have time to worry about it.

I dashed down the hall, warm cup of coffee in hand. I heard footsteps approaching behind me. As I swiveled around fast, Ben came running as some of my hot coffee spilled on my shirt.

"Hey, Lindsey, is everything all right?" he asked.

"Dammit, yes, I'm fine," I said, padding my sweater with a napkin.

"So sorry, I didn't mean to spook you," he said, taking a step closer. I sniffed his fruity-orange scent. His glare made a warm sensation flow through my body. My mouth became moist with saliva. Something snapped inside me and I stepped toward him.

Breathing in his breath, I became inundated with thoughts of his mouth on mine. I stood on my toes to reach him. He bent his head down lower. Our lips met, softly at first, then, I forced my tongue in his mouth. Ben reached his arms around me. His hand took hold of my coffee and placed it on his desk. It was the sweetest embrace I had experienced in a long time. I would've stayed there all night, locked in his arms. The crazy world I was living in kept at bay. Regrettably, the front door opened as a woman entered, making us break away from each other.

I tried to make myself look busy. The woman winked at me as she realized she had interrupted our kiss. The hair on my arms raised, my heart pounded. I looked away from Ben, avoiding his glance as he gave instructions to the woman who entered to sign in. Ben handed me my coffee back. I exited without looking at him.

"Bye," he yelled after me.

"Goodnight," I said, smiling to myself.

# 10

# Going Home

Back at my apartment, Matt was waiting for me. I sat on a stool at the kitchen island as we gulped down a slice of cold pizza.

"Why is this so cold?" I asked, tossing my slice back in the cardboard box.

"Sorry, you never called me to say when you'd be here, so I ordered it," Matt sputtered, darting my gaze.

"You could have at least left me more than two pieces. I haven't eaten much this week. And now I have to go take care of my parents." I rubbed the back of my neck as thoughts of kissing Ben filled my mind.

"Sorry, I'll order another one." Matts ears were turning red, something they did when he was embarrassed.

"Forget it, I'm not hungry anymore. And quit telling me you're sorry all the time!"

"I'm so—" His entire face turned a deep solferino color this time as I flashed him an obstinate gaze. We talked very little after the fight. I found my feelings for Ben validated somewhat. Matt knew all I was going through, yet, he had no way to comfort me. I no longer felt guilty about the kiss.

"Do you want me to come with you tonight?" he asked. His voice sounded as cold as the pizza.

"No." My voice was cool too. "Plus, I'm going to stop by the vet and check on Ginger. And, besides, don't you have to work tomorrow?" I reminded him.

"Yeah," he said, chewing his food like a cow.

"I have to jump in the shower and get going. Thanks for coming by." I stood and pecked him on the cheek.

"You sure you don't want to lie down and rest a little?"

*Translation: have a quickie.*

"I don't have time, Matt," I said sourly. Standing up, I stormed out of the room. Grabbed an overnight bag, threw some clothes in it and showered. By the time I had returned to the kitchen, Matt had taken off. He managed to leave me a note by the vase. He'd bought me flowers and placed them by my keys. They were beautiful. The aroma they delivered was perfect. There was a bunch of pink carnations, yellow daisies and purple hyacinths. But all I wanted was oranges. The note said he loved me and was sorry for the pain I was going through. I began sobbing. But, it wasn't from his act of kindness. I was simply spent. And the night had not yet begun.

Arriving at the veterinarian's clinic, I saw Carol's car still there. God, what day was it? I'd effectively lost track of time.

Carol lit up when I entered. She had freshly applied make-up. Gee, I wondered why?

"Lins! God, you've been having one hell of a week," she said, hugging me tight.

"Words cannot describe, babe," I agreed. Then I whispered in her ear, "So, you like Dr. Goldman?"

"No ring on his finger," she smirked. "Yet." I smacked her on her ass.

"Let's go see my baby," I said.

They were right about Ginger's improvement. Her movements were stiff, but the fact that she was moving freely on her own when I walked into her room gave me cause to celebrate. This time her voice made a meow whine loud and clear. The same way she'd do at home when she wanted food. Dr. Goldman gave me an update while I stroked her paws. She would be blind, naturally, in her left eye. The burn marks were superficial and no other permanent damage had been done. A full recovery, the best news I'd heard all day.

"Do you want me to come by tomorrow and visit her, or is Matt coming?" Carol asked. Something told me she'd drop by whether or not I needed her to.

"I'd love it if you came," I begged. "Matt and I aren't clicking at all right now," I said with a frown. Carol patted my back to show me support.

"No problem, I like it here," she said, speaking in a bubbly tone. She was definitely smitten with Dr. Goldman.

"I know you do. Did you hear that, Ginger? Carol will visit you tomorrow, okay?" Ginger's ears rose. We sat in silence for a while, the three of us. I looked at Carol, wanting to tell her about kissing Ben. But I didn't have the energy or the time. My parents needed me. So, we said our goodbyes. Ginger was in capable hands.

The drive to Coral Bay Nursing Home took twenty minutes. A sinking feeling occurred when I pulled in the parking lot. *This is where my dad was going to die.* It was a huge three-story building painted in pink. When I walked inside I saw a nice grassy park with benches set in the middle of the structure. Elevator music played through the walls. Get well baskets smothered the countertops. I signed in, got my guest-badge and rode the elevator to the third floor. His room number was 318, a name tag for Greg CarMichael displayed by his door.

When I peeked inside the dimly lit room, Mom was adjusting Dad's pillows. Dad swung his thin arms around Mom's even frailer appendages. They were already fighting. Such was the case with the two of them, even something as mundane as pillow placement caused a ruckus.

"I don't know what you're doing here!" Dad screamed, wide eyed and brows arched.

"Greg, stop fighting me. Your pillows need adjusting," Mom scolded him as if he had become a child. With that, I bent around the corner before they had seen me. I stood with my body against the wall and took a deep breath. Echoes of their fight about the placement of pillows vibrated through the hall. People walking by began to stare in the room, and at me.

"Miss, are you all right?" one of the nurses at the station asked. I motioned with my finger, pointing it at my chest.

Quickly, I responded. "Yes, I'm fine." I became embarrassed. I inhaled until I could feel my lungs full of air. Then, I breathed out.

"I'm looking for Greg CarMichael," I asked the nurse, using my best baby-kitten eyes.

"Right behind you, 318," she pointed with an agitated glance. "It takes all kinds," she said, shaking her head.

"Uh-huh," said another nurse nearby. I took the hint.

"Mom?" I asked, timidly walking in. The bony woman with the grey roots sprouting from her head mixed poorly with her colored black hair turned, her once emerald eyes now dull. Her eyes filled up with tears when she saw me. Mom's face wrinkled as she sighed. She had never looked worse.

"Lindsey, I'm so glad you're here," she cried. We embraced tightly and stood still for a while.

"It's okay," I said. "Everything will be all right." Even I didn't believe my words had any comfort to her. Mom released me and we turned our attention to the person who vaguely reminded me of my father, his hazel eyes glazed over. Clothed in a brown sweatshirt and baggy pants, Dad lifted his hands toward me. I ran to embrace him in bed. He allowed me. He returned my hug and patted my back. We all cried until he spoke.

"You're such a good girl, so pretty and you've always tried to help people." He stroked my hair delicately. "I'm glad you're my nurse." I peered at Mom and she shrugged. She had the 'what am I going to do?' expression on her face. I rested my chin on Dad's chest. My head bobbed up and down as he breathed the tobacco-stinking air in my direction, forcing me to sit up.

"Hi, Daddy," I chimed, happy to see him.

"Daddy? Who...who are you?" Dad shuddered as he moved away from me. His voice was shaky and frightened.

"Greg, it's Lindsey," Mom came to my defense. Dad wasn't buying it. He shook his head in insolence.

"It's me, Dad, your daughter, Lins, remember?" I addressed him head on. Something that had always worked in the past, but now it was losing its effect on him. Our eyes met and I refused to look away from him. "Do you understand, Dad? Can you see me now?" I felt a tingling in my chest.

"What are you jabbering about, lady! I see you." He grabbed my arm and pulled me closer. "I'm not blind you know. My eyes work just fine. My noodle gives me some trouble every once in a while, but I can tell that *you* are my Nurse Kelly." As Dad let go of my arm, Mom rose and began pacing around the room. This had to cease or Mom would end up having a heart attack.

"Okay, Dad. I'm your Nurse Kelly." I nodded to Mom. She collapsed back on her chair. She placed her hand on her head and watched as the two of us spoke.

"Damn straight you're my nurse! Don't you think I know my own nurse, when I see her? Glad we got that settled. Now everyone relax." Dad said, glancing at Mom. Mom closed her eyes and leaned on her knees with her elbows.

"All right, okay, Nurse Kelly is here to see you, Greg," she succumbed.

I smirked and nodded too. I pretended to take his pulse and he settled down. All was right with the world once more.

"Yeah, you should be happy my daughter Lindsey isn't here," he added. My head turned to look at Mom.

"Oh, Greg, don't start," Mom said.

She arched her back, ready for something seemingly unpleasant to occur. One quick gander at my dad and I knew at once what she was worried about.

He was going to spew to Nurse Kelly something Nurse Kelly already knew.

"Will you shut up, woman? All I ever hear from you are orders. Dear God! Kelly, I'm sure glad you're here to witness this." Dad focused on me—his eyes were all ablaze. I dutifully pretended to be Nurse Kelly. It was I who had to take my medicine now.

"Greg!" Mom tried again. I waved her off. It was no use stopping him once he started. It would prolong all the drama.

"Kelly, listen to this story. You won't believe it. Even I don't believe it and I was the one who lived through every single part." Dad scooted toward the edge of the bed near me. "My daughter Lindsey came straight out of college. She got her Master's degree in Social Work and she was all hoity-toity. She knew it all and was going to save the world. So stupid...I warned her. I told her to become a lawyer like me, but she didn't listen." Dad rolled his head around, stretching his neck and shoulders as if he was about to tell a scary tale at a gathering around a camp fire.

"What did she do?" I egged him on. The quicker I removed the bandage—.

"I'll tell you. The first case she was assigned to was a ten-year-old black girl who lived in the poorest part of town. Apparently, the girl's father had been," Dad squeezed his wrinkled face so he could whisper, "abusing her, you know, sexually," Dad whispered, looking out toward the hall to see if anyone had heard. He angrily tossed his arm around when he saw a staff member gaze in. Blinking my eyes, I reached out to hold his hand steady.

"Then what happened?" I asked. Mom exhaled behind me. Maybe, he had been reciting this like a broken record to her. Hell, I would be addicted to Vicodin too if that was the case. Dad was the sweetest man I've ever known. But, he became ruthless in the courtroom. Was this the persona we were left with until the end? I started having difficulty swallowing.

"She did her job. Lindsey got the girl the hell away from that man and placed her into a foster care home," he said and became quiet, lost in thought or he'd forgotten the story all together. I'd hope for the latter. Unfortunately, he broke out in a fit of laughter instead and my eyes swelled. I had left one crazy place at home for another here.

"Gregory, it's not funny," Mom chastised, which made him laugh harder. Mom stood on the opposite side of the bed. Using both her hands, she grabbed his face, turning it toward her. "Please stop," she pleaded with a shaky voice.

"No, no, let go of me. Kelly needs to know this in case Lindsey ever tries to do something crazy," Dad commanded. Showing the whites of his eyes, he jabbed his finger in Mom's face.

Mom tried her best, but I could tell from the look in her eyes she was spent. The three of us were on the roller coaster ride until its conclusion. Good thing there had been a bin placed in the room if anyone felt the need to vomit.

"You see the way she treats me, Kelly? I'm glad I'm here with you and out of that house. Where was I? Oh yeah, my daughter Lindsey. Well, my bright know-it-all daughter, who has always listened to me. She always took my advice. Except when it came to her career, she didn't want to follow in my footsteps. She decided to work as a therapist because she took a bunch of psychology courses. What a waste of talent! She could have had her own law firm. Hell, she could have been a judge on the Supreme Court, she was that brilliant. But, no, she graduated and started working as a case manager, a grunt, for the state. They pay you nothing and expect you to work twenty-four hours a day, understaffed and overwhelmed with cases.

"Oh, Greg," Mom sobbed.

I felt the rivulets of tears flowing down my face—unable to stop the dam. Bending my head, I kept my eyes on the floor. I knew what was coming. All I wanted was to go home and be with Ginger.

"Don't you cry, Kelly," Dad said softly. "Lindsey tried her best." He bobbed his head. "But the work she did, made her go insane."

A sob escaped from my mouth. I covered my lips with my hand.

"Yes, there was a young girl...what was her name?"

"Angel," I said.

"Yes, that's the one. That case did Lindsey in. Lindsey was the one who had to be placed in the loony bin." Dad circled his forefinger around his head. Silence devoured the room once more. Dad then added, "It was a while before they allowed her to practice again. And you know who saved her stupid ass? Me, yeah," he said, full of pride. "I used to be good friends with the District Attorney, I was a lawyer, you know," he nodded toward me as I lifted my head and allowed the tears to flow at will. "And we helped get her out of that horrible mess. It was because I threatened to sue the state board! Ah, what a shame, she had such promise—a Harvard graduate, top of the class. She was published before she had even graduated. Then, she blew it!" Dad's eyes turned misty. "That's why she has to see a shrink. She's nuts herself." Dad's forehead and chin glistened with sweat. He became lost in thought.

I numbly rose and looked at him for a bit—reaching for the box of tissues. A hearty blow escaped from my nose as I handed Mom a few of the tissues also. Evading my dad's gaze, I entered his restroom, closed the door and threw cold water on my face. Mom could still be heard crying. Dad chastised her for weeping. They began to argue total nonsense as I glared into the mirror's reflection.

# 11

## Foster Care Center

### July 14th, 2007

"That's it! I am never dieting again!" Maggie screamed as she threw her plate she had just eaten for dinner in the trash.

"Was it that bad?" I laughed at her.

"Lindsey, I don't think 'bad' is the correct word to describe it."

"No?"

"No," she said curtly, "Bad, would've assumed I was able to eat it in the first place. I couldn't even chew this piece of crap. It had no taste, no flavor, no substance. Shit, I'll have to join a gym and work out. And, Lins, you know how much I hate exercising." Maggie clenched her jaw and made a fist punch in the air with her hands.

"You can join my gym. There are a ton of cute looking guys who work out there," I offered.

"Really? Have you ever dated any of them?" she asked.

"Good God no!" I giggled. "You don't date those guys, you sleep with them."

"What? Why?" She turned her face upright with a smile.

"Let me put it this way. The larger the pecs on a man's chest, the smaller his brain will be. Oh, and he'll have a huge ego too," I added.

"What about the size of his—? You know," she smirked.

"I found no correlation to that, except, maybe hand size. But, that's not always the case." I frowned.

Maggie always had a way of making the evening shift go much faster when the two of us were working alone. During the day the place was in total chaos with people coming and going, screaming, fighting. It was commonplace for the police to be there. I liked her from day one. I knew we'd be good friends and she showed me the ropes fast and efficiently. The evening shift had consisted of answering phone calls and filling out incident reports. Unless there was an emergency, we stayed until midnight.

"Uh oh, I think there's trouble." Maggie motioned with her head to the front door. Our boss walked in with his tie loose around his neck and his hair disheveled.

"Hi, Paul, what's up?" I asked.

"Lindsey, I need you. I just got off the phone with the police. They want you at Angel Fisher's foster care home," Paul said.

"Why? What's wrong?" I chewed on my lip.

"They wouldn't tell me. Are you okay going there by yourself, because we have to have two people here at all times?"

"Sure, no problem," I said, grabbing my purse. Paul walked me to the door and Maggie mouthed, "Good luck."

Police cars filled the streets. I had to show my identification badge repeatedly in order to just get near the house. I was ordered to stay put for over an hour. After a while, a policeman signaled me to move in his direction. As I made my way through the crowd that had gathered, I saw it. An ambulance gurney with a body placed in the bag covered the front side walk.

"This way, ma'am," the policeman said.

My feet wouldn't move. I'd never seen a dead person before. The flickering lights made me dizzy.

"What's going on?" I asked.

"Are you Lindsey CarMichael of Foster Care Services?"

"Yes."

"I was told to have you identify the body. You were assigned to Angel Fisher's case, correct?"

I gaped. I took a few steps backward. My ears thumped with the beating of my heart. I saw three other teenage girls huddled together on the front porch. The foster care mother was screaming, making scurrilous claims for the whole neighborhood to hear. But, I couldn't get past looking at the body bag. The policeman signaled once again for me to follow him. I plodded toward him as he lifted the yellow tape for me to slouch under to the other side.

Every step I moved closer to the bag, my hands started to flutter. My mouth dried up. The policeman gazed at me with wide eyes and said, "Are you ready?" The officer had undoubtedly done this a million times, but this was my first. My knees were about to give way.

I nodded to him.

People who were standing by us stopped talking. The three girls had tears in their eyes. I focused on the bag. I needed to get this over with quickly.

A female paramedic performed the honors. With her dark blue latex gloves, she unzipped the front of the bag and I saw Angel Fisher's face. Her eyes were closed, hair matted. The front of her shirt was soaked with bloodstains.

"Is this your client?" the policeman asked.

"Huh?" My eyes were transfixed on her, then I answered. "Yes, this is Angel Fisher." A sudden chill hit me to the very core. I wanted answers. "How did this happen?" I asked the policeman. He shrugged and told me to talk to the detectives on the porch. He turned and hollered up toward two men in plain suits.

"It's her, Angel Fisher, I have confirmation," he said callously.

"No, no, no, my baby did nothing!" the foster mother said.

I approached the porch and saw the two detectives interviewing a teenage boy, the foster care mother's son. I'd always liked him. He seemed so sweet when I came around to visit. I couldn't imagine he had something to do with this. I was wrong.

Before I could say a word, the boy was being handcuffed and read his Miranda rights by one of the detectives. His mother went crazy and fell to the floor kicking and trying to hold onto his legs. I leaned back in the doorframe to get out of the way. That's when he caught my eye. He smiled from ear to ear, as if thanking me for offering up Angel Fisher to him on a silver platter. I knew what had happened without being told.

"You son of a bitch!" I said, running toward him and began punching him in the face. He lowered his head and I pulled his hair while he screamed. I kicked him in the groin. When the police pulled me off him, I saw that his face was covered in blood from my attack. "You're a dead man! You hear me? You're fucking dead!" I kept yelling as I was being placed in the back seat of a cop car, handcuffed. All I could see was a blinding white light that the police had set up for the crime scene. I sat there for hours sobbing and watching people stare at me.

At the end, one of the detectives opened the front door on the passenger side. He calmed me down. Told me the entire story I already knew. He said that they would drive me home in a few minutes and I would not be charged with anything. The entire time he spoke, I simply watched the lifeless body of Angel Fisher out on display for people to watch. It was an evening's entertainment. I became catatonic.

Dad opened the door as the police walked me up the steps to my house. The two of them exchanged words. I said nothing. Mom became hysterical as usual. Dad asked me if I wanted to talk. I shook my head and went to use the bathroom. I saw Mom's Vicodin pills, freshly refilled. I swallowed as many as I could until blackness engulfed me.

# 12

# Sun Valley Center 2007

## Day One

I woke up in a haze in the back seat of a car. Tree branches cast long shadows as they flew by the window. I glanced at the time and it was four o' clock in the morning. Dad must have been driving all night long.

"Where are we going?" I asked.

"Thank God, you're up," he breathed a sigh of relief.

"I'm taking you to the best mental hospital in North Florida. It's run by the state," Dad told me. "It's the best option you have, if you ever want to return to work."

"Why? What did I do?"

"You don't remember?" he asked.

"I remember throwing up in the bathroom."

"You were trying to take all of your mother's Vicodin pills and I stuck my finger down your throat."

"Oh, God, now I remember." I cringed, thinking about all the chaos that had ensued.

"It wasn't that bad, Lindsey. You were traumatized, do you hear me? When people ask, you say you were beside yourself with grief." He continued to mutter, "Beside yourself with grief."

I looked up in the rear view mirror at my dad. What was I grieving over? His face wrinkled, deep in thought. Everything was slowly coming back to me, but in flashes.

"Where's Mom?"

"She couldn't...she has a hard time dealing with her feelings. You know that already. She's too sensitive and fragile. I told her you needed to be calm and clear, when you sign yourself in this place. Your mother was just plain hysterical. You know how she gets."

"Wait a minute. I am signing myself in? For what? Dad, they could keep me as long as they wanted." I leaned over the back of my dad's seat. Anxiety filled me to the brim.

"Lindsey, if you behave and act normal, you'll be out in three days at the most. Honey, you were acting crazy when you got to the scene of the crime. You threatened that boy's life as he was being taken into custody. You attacked him physically as well. People heard you. The police heard you. There's going to be a state-wide investigation on how that family became eligible for foster care. They're going to be looking for a scapegoat and I don't want it to be you, understand?"

I curled up into a ball in the back seat, crying inconsolably. I tugged at the pillow someone had left there and went back to sleep.

After an hour, Dad woke me up. He was about to pull into the Sun Valley Center's parking lot. He wanted me to put on makeup and fix my hair.

"Be calm and together, but don't be a wallflower either." He was more nervous than I had thought. The Vicodin kept me in a foggy state for the most part. I'd worked in mental hospitals during my internship. I knew what they were like. I kept telling myself it wouldn't be that bad.

"I know the drill, Dad. Okay? This is so humiliating," I said.

"If you had done what I told you and become a lawyer, none of this would have happened," he said snidely.

"Shut the hell up, will you? I have to think about what I'm going to say. Making those comments, at a time like this doesn't help, understand?" I raged.

Dad gave me a look I would not soon forget. I had never yelled at him before, not like that anyway. I looked in my facial powder compact mirror. The crazy person inside had emerged. Someone had dressed me in sweatpants and an old jersey, probably Mom. My hair needed brushing so I pulled it back and braided it.

"Ready?" Dad was getting impatient, restless. "Come on, I still have a long drive home and it's getting late."

"All right, let's go."

Police let us in and showed us to the waiting room. Dad filled out all the paperwork while I nervously played with my braided hair. I should have been the one filling it out. The woman in charge of admitting me took the papers and told me to leave all personal belongings with Dad. *God, I was going to be strip-searched!* Dad gave me a stern look and we said our goodbyes. The door locked shut behind me.

"You can sit here," the woman said sanctimoniously in the padded room. Two other rather large women stood on either side of me. My eyes bulged out of their sockets and my lips began to tremble. If I wasn't full of trepidation before I had entered the room, I perceptibly was now.

"My name is Ellen and I'm going to ask you a few questions, okay?" She had full length curly brown hair that fell over her red-trimmed glasses each time she looked down.

I nodded.

She looked over my file and quickly glanced up at me. "You're a licensed social worker?"

"Yes." I wasn't throwing out any crumbs for her to pick up.

"Tell me why you're here."

"I tried to hurt myself by taking my mother's Vicodin pills."

"How many pills?"

"The whole bottle."

"I see," Ellen said, pushing her hair back. "Did you want to die?"

"No, it was more a cry for help." I flat-out lied. *Three days, please.*

"All right, Lindsey, before we take you back to the living quarters, we need you to remove all of your clothes." Ellen acted like it was no big deal. The three of them pulled a curtain around me, watched as I disrobed. They were wearing rubber gloves. Each piece of clothing I removed was taken by one of the woman and patted down. They had inspected the seams in my sweatshirt at the neck, wrists, and also my bra. My pant legs were checked out as well as shoes and socks. It was then when I realized I had my period.

"I don't want to remove my underwear. It's that time of the month, you know?" I hunched my shoulders.

"I'm sorry. But we have to make sure everyone will be safe. Just pull them down quickly and it will all be over."

I bent over and did as I was told, exposing myself, my blood, to three strange women. I must have been crazy to allow this insanity to continue. It triggered thoughts of Angel fending for herself as her own father and that boy tore away her innocence. Tears filled my eyes, all the anger, rage and humiliation, exploded in that second.

"Get me the fuck out of here!" I screamed, lunging at Ellen. Someone slammed my head against the wall as a 'Code Red Admitting' siren filled the walls. Within seconds, scattered voices and hands held me and saw me naked. I closed my eyes and screamed for Angel.

"I'm so sorry, Angel! Please forgive me."

I felt a prick of a needle, the pressure of medicine flow through me as I fell asleep.

## 13

## Day Two

Sounds of people laughing and the ruffling of plastic cups circled around me. I thought I was dreaming at first until I tried to turn on my side and found I couldn't move. My eyes snapped open. The corked tile ceiling with a million tiny eyes stared back at me.

Strapped to four points of the bed, I began to tremble. The bed was covered in rubber sheets and I had urinated. I had on a hospital gown and it felt wet. How long had I been here?

People flitted by my door-less room. Desperately, I tried to get orientated to my surroundings. My nose itched and the straps refused me access. I had pushed the envelope too far this time.

"Can anyone help me? Hello?" I found my voice.

A black man with a grey hat and beard peeked in.

What could I do? I was defenseless.

"I'll tell them you're awake, hold on," he said with a murky voice. *What the hell did they give me?*

"Thank you," I hollered, yanking at my straps.

A short scrawny-looking woman with red hair appeared in my doorway. She wore a necklace with her badge and keys. Her eyes gave me a quick look over before she spoke.

"Hi, Lindsey, how do you feel right now?" she asked, wrinkling her forehead above her nose.

"I'm fine," I said composedly, "can you please unstrap me?"

"Yes, I can. I'm just waiting on another tech to assist me. We have to do this in pairs."

"Thank you." I gazed at her name tag. "Your name is Mandy?"

"Yes," she smiled. "Henry, can you come in here?" She signaled with her tiny arm. There was no way Mandy did any physical restraining. When Henry dangled his head in the door way, I knew why Mandy wouldn't have to. He must have been seven feet tall.

"Everything all right?" he asked me.

"Uh-huh, I'm better now."

"This is how it works, Lindsey. We take off one strap at a time, okay?" Henry glided pass Mandy to the front left side of my bed. "I don't want any trouble from you. Today is a fresh start."

"I understand. You won't even know I'm here." I smiled prudently.

Henry removed the strap from my left hand. I slowly pulled it over to scratch my nose. Mandy watched my every move. He then crossed over to my right side and removed my right hand strap. I pulled my elbows to stretch my arms.

"Thank you," I said.

"You want to sit up? Here, I'll help you." Henry reached behind my back and used his arms to pull me up. I rubbed my hands on my face and tried to shake off the fuzzy feeling I had.

"How do you feel, Lindsey?" Mandy asked once more.

"Groggy, out of it." I shook my head.

"The medication will wear off soon, don't worry," she said.

"Now I will undo the left foot," Henry continued on his way. I curled it under me as soon as it was released. I moved the same way with my right leg. Although I was free, I didn't want to leave the room just yet. I sat on the edge of the bed listening to people talk in the hall. Henry said I needed to get up and walk around a little bit. As soon as my feet hit the floor, I slipped back down on the bed.

"I'm too dizzy. I can't walk yet." I shook my head and tried to focus my vision on their faces. Images were blurry and I got a headache.

"The doctor is making his rounds now. Why don't you stay here until he checks you out?" Mandy said.

"Okay, yeah," I nodded. The truth was I wanted to be alone. I began to get angry, thinking that they had over-medicated me on purpose. My limbs were raggedy. And I knew my little stunt when I was admitted had made my stay at this lovely hotel at least a few days longer.

"And who might you be, lovely lady?" Dr. Peterson entered looking at his chart.

"Oh, just another person to keep these people employed," I joked.

"I'm glad your sense of humor is still intact." He gave me a warm smile, took my blood pressure, and listened to my heartbeat. He couldn't have been sweeter. He took a blood and urine sample and told me to drink lots of water to flush out the sedative they gave me. I asked him if I could have my clothes back and he said he'd talk to the nurse.

"What was the medicine they used to sedate me?" I attempted to ask offhandedly.

"Let me check your chart," Dr. Peterson said as he thumbed through the pages. "Ah, yes, you were administered ten milligrams of haloperidol mixed with sixty milligrams promethazine."

"Wow, that was a strong dose! Isn't it supposed to be fifty milligrams of promethazine, not sixty?" I tilted my head.

"Yes, but when a staff member is attacked, exclusively in admitting, well, they tend to go for a very strong dose." He lowered his head but kept his eyes on me.

"Try to walk around a bit. Your blood pressure is good."

"Yeah, I will," I said. I waited until he left the room and then I stood again, feeling better.

I peered out in the hall and saw people sitting in a common area. No one was really talking to each other. They all were simply waiting, for what, I had no idea. I noticed the water cooler and braved leaving the confines of my room. Mandy gave me a nice smile. I must have downed four glasses of water. The plastic cups might as well have been thimbles. Everyone started to get up and stood in line.

"What's going on?" I asked Mandy.

"It's dinner time, but you're on level 'R' which means restricted to the unit. So, a tray will be sent here for you."

I wanted some alone time, well I got some alone time, with crappy food. Wait a minute, it was dinner time? That meant I had been knocked out all day long! They were not allowed to do that. No sedative should last longer than four hours. Mine had lasted for ten or eleven.

I approached the nurse's station and talked to Mandy.

"How you doing, Lindsey? I have your clothes if you want to change into them."

"Thank you, yes, I'm freezing in here." I reached into the bag and Mandy watched me remove my belongings and took the bag away.

"Can I ask you something?"

"Sure."

"Why did they sedate me so long?"

"I don't know. Did you talk to the doctor about this?"

"Yes, but I think they overdosed me. Didn't a staff member notice I was sleeping all day long?" My lips pursed.

"We checked in on you every fifteen minutes as per protocol. You were snoring your head off so we knew you were okay." Mandy raised her brows. She knew what I was hinting at and I could tell she didn't enjoy my accusation.

"When do I see my psychiatrist? What is his name?"

"Everything is on the board above the station." She pointed up and turned around ignoring me, busying herself.

I had missed my psychiatrist's appointment. Heat flushed through my veins, I was so angry. It had been at 9:00 a.m. Also, I was assigned to a woman not a man: Dr. Sharon Hingley.

# 14

# Day Three

Since I had slept for over twelve hours, I'd thought I wouldn't be able to rest much during the night. On the contrary, I was still exhausted and weary. I made it a point to tell the night staff, after Mandy left, I wanted to make my doctor's appointment.

"Please make sure I'm awake and on time," I said.

"No problem, we wake everyone up at six in the morning," a male staff member said.

"You didn't today," I said under my breath.

"What was that?" he challenged.

"Nothing, good night."

Wake up time was at six. I moved into a room with another young woman whose name was Grace. She was short, hefty and didn't make much eye contact. I got the feeling that she had enjoyed having the room all to herself and was not a happy camper that I moved in. So, I kept out of her way. Showering the piss, blood and sweat off me from the past three days, I began to feel like a person again.

Something vaguely disguised as scrambled eggs was served on my tray, still restricted to the unit. I forced it down with a carton of orange juice. I didn't want any more attention. Becoming a wallflower was the best way to stay out of trouble here.

"Lindsey CarMichael?" a female staff called out for me.

"Yes, I'm here," I answered, running toward her.

The woman and a male staff member walked me through a series of doors down the hall. All of them had to be locked and unlocked as we passed by. Whoever designed this place wasn't thinking ahead of all the keys demanded in order to move twenty feet. As we approached our destination, I saw many plants and welcoming chairs to sit upon. Posh tan-colored throw rugs lay over ugly worn out carpets. A woman sat behind a marble desk, the queen doctor, I presumed. During the entire five minutes of my therapy session, she had looked up once. The two staff attendees stood outside with the door opened. They weren't taking any more chances.

"Hello, Ms. CarMichael, how are you today?"

"Much better, thank you." I smiled.

"I understand you had an incident at admitting. Can you tell me about that?" Sharon scribbled incessantly. I had no idea I was so fascinating.

"I was very upset as you can imagine. I overreacted to the situation. A client of mine was just killed and I was in shock. I'm much better now." I almost added that I want to go home, but I thought that'd be pushing my luck.

"Your story has made the national news." She glanced at me. "How do you feel about that?"

"It doesn't surprise me. I expected it to. It was a horrible, tragic situation." I remained cool and collected.

"Do you feel like hurting yourself?"

"No."

"Are you feeling anxious or sad?"

"No."

"Let me guess, you want to go home. Correct?"

"Yes."

"Give me twenty-four hours of stable behavior and we'll see about tomorrow. Thank you."

I rose to my feet and began to leave. Curiosity forced me to ask, even though I shouldn't have. "Doctor, as you are aware of my background, I know that there are limits placed on dosage amounts of drugs that can be administered to patients."

Sharon stopped writing but kept looking down.

"I believe I was given more than the appropriate dosage when I was admitted. My father, who is an attorney, will be calling you shortly regarding this issue. Thank you."

I heard a slight laugh on my way out the door. As soon as I returned to my unit, I saw I was no longer on level 'R' and went to use the patients' phone. I called home, but Mom didn't pick up. So, I called my dad's office instead.

"Lins, how are you?" he asked, with a desperate tone in his voice.

"I'm fine, now. But I had a rough entrance. They over-sedated me, Dad. I was out of it for eleven hours at least. I woke up the next day at dinner time, strapped down on a rubber sheeted bed."

"Sweet Jesus!" he shouted.

"Then, I met the psychiatrist and she's a nut job. If she's running this place, she should be fired." One of the staff members who heard me say this snickered when I looked at her.

"I can't talk long. Just get me out of here, okay?"

"They are raising hell about Angel's case, honey. Are you sure you don't want to rest for a couple of days?"

"You don't rest in here, Dad," I said, as I watched a woman pick her nose and twirl the booger around in her finger. I turned around so I wasn't facing her.

"All right, I'll get you out."

"Thanks, I love you and tell Mom I love her too." My entire body started to relax.

"I will."

I hung up the phone and went back toward my bedroom. Mandy called me back to the nurses' station. What now?

"Lindsey, I have your medication." I felt like I was moving in slow motion. She couldn't have said my name. I approached the station as Mandy held out a tiny cup of water and a plastic one for pills.

"What is this?" I asked.

"Doctor has ordered you an anti-depressant Zoloft 10 milligrams and 0.25 milligrams of Valium." She smiled her usual cheery face.

"You have to be kidding me." My arms crossed my chest.

"No, the order just came through."

"I'm not taking it," I said in a high pitched voice.

"You're refusing your medication?" Mandy squinted with a sudden stiffening posture.

"I am," I confirmed, watching her to see how she would react. Other patients were watching too.

"I will mark it in the charts."

"You do that," I sneered.

Footsteps approached me from behind. My roommate Grace jumped in front of me. She had a comb stuck in her hair. Her face was bright and excited.

"Oh, there's going to be trouble. I can feel it." She bounced from foot to foot.

"Grace, leave her alone," Mandy ordered. I wanted to call my dad back.

I spun around to use the phone again and saw the same black man with a grey hat and beard who had seen me when I had woken up yesterday. Now he was staring at me. This time, he blew me a kiss. I recoiled and hoped someone had seen him. No luck.

"Time for group," Henry announced.

Chairs were placed in a circle in the living quarter. I sat down as far away as I could from everyone. Henry went around the room and asked how each person was feeling. Most people said fine or bored, until it was Grace's turn.

"I feel angry!" she said.

"Why is that?" Henry asked.

"Why does my roommate get to skip her medication but I have to take mine, huh?" She tapped her feet in protest.

If there was going to be trouble, Grace wanted to be the cause of it. I gazed around the room and felt all eyes peering back at me. Heat filled my cheeks.

"Grace, isn't one of your goals to focus on yourself and not other patients?" Henry came to my defense, sort of.

"I am! She's living in my bedroom and I think it's best if she takes her meds too," Grace said adamantly. A couple of moans and groans were heard at a low volume. They were just loud enough for certain large men to inch their way closer, nonchalantly. I laughed out loud. This was a mistake of a lifetime.

"Calm down, Grace, would you like to walk with Jill and Mike?" Both of them were staff members.

"Yes, I would." Grace said glaring at me. *Wonderful, my roommate is a psychopath!* After group ended, I moved to another room with suicidal Cindy. She was my type of roommate, quiet, and merely wanted to hurt herself, not me.

The food in the dining hall was much more edible, even if I still had no access to caffeine. We had to eat in long rows of tables. I chose the end seat closest to the door just in case someone wanted to mess with me.

Walking back to my room, I heard wails of screams and moans coming from the hall. I peeked into the door-less room that I first stayed in and saw Grace strapped down to the bed. I shouldn't have looked. It made the whole situation worse.

"I'm gonna kill you, bitch!" she hollered at me.

"Sleep well," I taunted.

"Lindsey, go back to your room. It's time for bed," Mandy ordered. I turned to her and nodded with a gentle smile. I went to sleep hoping tomorrow would be my last day in this nut house.

# 15

# Day Four

I noticed on the schedule that today was a visiting day for family. Instantly, I called my dad to tell him. His secretary told me he already knew and was on his way to see me. I called my mom. Still no answer, she was with him. Something told me I just had to wait a few more hours and I could go home.

The same two staff members from yesterday walked me to see my wonderful psychiatrist, Dr. Sharon Hingley. I joyfully took my seat across from her desk.

"You seem to be in a good mood today." She looked up at me, crossing her arms.

"I am. Thank you for noticing. I'd like to go home today." I didn't beat around the bush.

"I see. However, I asked you to give me twenty-four hours of stable behavior and—"

"I did," I interrupted her.

She smiled and tilted her head lower. "Please do not interrupt me again." She exhaled. "The staff noted on your chart that you refused the medication I ordered you to take."

"I—"

She placed her hand toward my face, palm up.

"Also, it was written that you provoked another patient while she was strapped in four points," she said sitting back, waiting for a response.

My stomach quivered and I pursed my lips. She wasn't going to let me leave. The idea of staying here one more day killed me. I placed my hand on my face and stared at the floor.

"You're right," I agreed. "I did all those things. But, I'm not going to be on medication when I leave, so what's the point of starting it now? And as for childishly teasing Grace, I will apologize as soon as I see her. I know how humiliating that can be when you're exposed like that," I said with steely eyes glaring at her. I wanted her to flinch, show an ounce of being nervous. But Sharon gave me nothing.

"Tell me about the night Angel Fisher was killed," she said coolly.

I went numb. I hadn't expected her to bluntly say something like that. Her eyes watched my body language. I started to fidget in my chair.

"It was terrible," I began. "When I arrived at the scene, she...she was in a body bag. I had to identify her for the police." I straightened myself in my chair.

"Did they tell you what happened?" she asked.

For the past four days I had been blocking it out of my mind. I swallowed a bottle of pills to get it out of my mind. If I wanted to leave this place, I had to remember. I had to remember all of it.

"Yes, they told me." I took a deep breath and exhaled. "According to the other girls who were also placed at the home—they said, the son would come into their rooms at night and take turns raping each one of them." Tears trickled down my nose. "The girls said, if it wasn't your turn, you had to help hold down the girl whose turn it was."

"God," Dr. Hingley whimpered.

"They said they all told the foster care mother. But she refused to believe them. And they weren't allowed to talk about it or they'd get punished. Everyone fell in line except for Angel. She was done being abused and took a kitchen knife with her to bed. When the boy went for her, she stabbed him in the arm. He grabbed his dad's gun and shot her. Case closed and it was all my fault."

"No, you couldn't have known. You have to forgive yourself."

It was then I sobbed. I cried for an hour. Sharon came over and sat by me. I didn't think I'd ever forgive myself, but her gesture, her words helped.

I went through the motions of the day. I had lunch, apologized to Grace and ceded to being institutionalized for quite a while.

Visiting hours started and I waited for my parents to arrive. My heart sank as Dad showed up alone. We walked over to the far end of the living quarters and sat down.

"Where's Mom?"

"She's having a very hard time dealing with all of this."

"*She's* having a hard time? I'm not partying down here either, you know? Mom won't even answer the phone when I call!"

"Take it easy, honey." Dad bent down and held my hands. He looked tired. His eyes had dark circles under them.

"What's going to happen now?" I asked.

"It's time for me to raise some hell and get you out of here," he smiled.

"Really?"

"Yep, I brought the papers signed by my friend Judge Kulm for your immediate release and an investigation of what happened to you, when you were admitted. Though, mind you, it's a last resort. I just plan to threaten them first," he smirked, raising his eyebrows.

I stood and hugged my dad as hard as I could. Fortunately for Sharon, he didn't have to make good on his threat. She was glad to get rid of me.

It took us four hours to drive home. Mom greeted us by the door. I forced a smile to placate Dad. But I was angry at her. At least the nightmare was over.

# 16

# Letting Go (Present Day)

After I had rinsed my face off from crying in the restroom, I stepped back inside Dad's room at the nursing home. Dad froze as his thinning eyebrows became one and his mouth opened. Three wrinkles appeared above his forehead. He recognized me. I was no longer Nurse Kelly.

"Dad?" I asked tentatively.

"Lindsey! Honey, I'm so glad to see you. When did you get here?" he said ecstatically, opening his arms wide for me to hug him.

"Just now." I held him until visiting hours were over. I kissed him on the head as he drifted off to sleep.

Mom talked my ear off when we got back to the house. She wrung her hands compulsively one over the other. They appeared dried and chapped. In fact, her whole body was rail-thin. She reminded me of Carrie Warner, but much older. We plopped down on the living room sofa and drank tea.

"Do you want some cookies? I think I have some in the pantry." Mom jumped up.

"No, Mom, please sit down. You're making me dizzy and you need to rest," I claimed. Out of sheer exhaustion, she complied. We both kept to our thoughts. Sounds of the central air flickered on as the house grew warmer. I randomly glanced at the mantel above the fireplace. It displayed pictures of holidays, me as a cheerleader and my graduation from college. It all seemed like a lifetime ago. I wished I had a sibling.

"How are things with Matt?" Mom spoke, breaking the silence.

"Not great, I'm afraid," I said, turning to face her, "I think we are growing apart."

"What? No, come on, Lindsey. Don't you think you can try harder? He stood by you after you shared your past with him. I think that must say something."

"You know, you're right, Mom. He did stand by me after he found out how crazy I was, but he's been treating me like shit ever since!" I fumed.

"Don't talk like that around me. You know I hate curse words. You sound just like your father."

"Well, goddammit, shit, fuck me then!" I hollered. Mom threw her arms up in the air, her eyes piercing daggers through me. "At least Dad took care of me in the nut house," I continued. "Why didn't you ever answer the phone when I called? Did you think all the crazy" (I air-quoted with my fingers) "would rub off on you?"

Mom leaped to her feet and moved toward the stairs to the second floor. I followed, full of rage. She wasn't going to get away with it this time. I had nothing to lose.

"I'm going to bed, leave me alone. How dare you come home and treat me like this, after the week I had dealing with your father? You're an ungrateful little snob." Mom turned half-way up the stairs and glared down at me. "We gave you everything we had—this beautiful house, the best schools, clothes, toys, you name it. All it ended up doing was spoiling you, making you think the world acts that way. Well, Lindsey, sorry honey, the world doesn't owe you a dime."

"You didn't answer my question." I looked at my mom with my eyes bulging out of their sockets. "Why, Mom? I had to be dragged from the scene of the crime by policemen. Some of them I still have to work with. I hurt myself because of all the pain. You knew I was terrified to be in that place." I rose to meet her on the stairs. "I spent most of my time closed off in my room."

"Didn't they have things for you to do—groups? Therapy?" Mom countered.

Laughing pathetically, I replied, "My groups consisted of dodging snot that a schizoid woman flicked after she picked her nose. One man there smiled at me and tried to trap me alone several times. Another woman, well, she simply wanted to beat the shit out of me. I have no idea why. And as for therapy, that was a joke. And we all know how wonderful the great and powerful Dr. Sharon

Hingley was, don't we? She most likely billed me twice her normal rate."

"I had no idea it was that bad." Mom shook her head.

"But most of all, you know how much I felt responsible for that poor little girl's death," I sobbed, tears stung my eyes. Silence covered the room like a blanket. Then, it was stripped away and I understood. "You blame me for letting it happen, don't you?" I narrowed my eyes.

"I never said that," she retorted.

"You didn't have to say it. You thought I got what I deserved. So, you let me take my medicine. I had determined that hell-hole was fit for foster care for Angel. Three other girls were placed there as well—all from my neglectful recommendation. They became victims of my mistake. So, you abandoned me because I humiliated the great CarMichael name, that's always been your way. Neat, tidy and perfect or else, you're banished."

Mom's lips narrowed to a single ruled line. She and I stood our ground. My unflinching stare against her guilty one—until she pivoted in defeat and stomped upstairs—leaving me like she had always done in the past. I might as well have been talking to a wall. It was just her and Dad against the world now. Until I produced an heir to the mighty throne, I would be invisible.

Trudging with my overnight bag, I went to the room I had spent most of my life in. While Mom and Dad had always slept upstairs with the two other guest rooms, I loved being on the ground floor. Guess it was easier to escape when I wanted to sneak out with a boy or go to a party. They never knew I had much more of a past than they thought and I liked it that way. Mom's concern was I never got pregnant. Other than that, we stayed out of each other's lives.

To Dad, I had always been his precious little prodigy. With an IQ of 190, my prospects were unlimited. Naturally, Dad wanted me to follow him and become a lawyer and a judge. Every Ivy League College offered me a full-scholarship. In my senior year of high school, I took a psychology class and I was hooked. Perturbed, but understanding once he saw my passion, Dad accepted my decision on one condition: I was to be the best in my field. And I was, until my very first case. He forgave me for my ten-year-old client's death. But, I was never mentioned to his friends and colleagues ever again. So, I let go of the thought of ever becoming wonderful in my work.

Dad's friends found me a great lawyer. They were able to prove that I wasn't to blame for the death of Angel. It turned out that I had done everything by the books when I checked out the foster care home. There were never any records of violence or neglect and they were a churchgoing family—well known in their community. So, I didn't lose my state license and was able to continue practicing social work.

However, I handed in my letter of resignation at the Foster Care Center. I went back to school to get my doctorate degree so I could open my own practice. I performed a large amount of intern work which paid nothing and attended classes in the evening. Basically, I worked from sun up until sun down. I ran myself ragged, still running from ghosts. Living with Mom and Dad was okay, but not great. I wanted my independence back. And when I met Matt, I decided it was time to move out. Lo and behold, I found out Dr. Sharon Hingley had left Sun Valley Center and started her own practice.

She was floored when I met with her. Her caseload was in full bloom and she needed help. I dropped out of school after two years of studying. I didn't have my doctorate, but as long as I was working under someone who had one, and more, I could start providing therapy sessions.

Now, I managed a few twisted individuals under the close scrutiny of her. We'd had mutual animosity for one another since the beginning. But, somehow it managed to work. Dad always had said, "It's good to have friction at work. It keeps you on your toes." At present, my toes were extremely sore.

Then, the bottom fell out when Dad started to forget things. His friends at the law firm covered as long as they could for him. Eventually, he messed up a huge case involving one of their top clients. Mom and I forced him to see a neurologist. The doctor confirmed our worst fears. He had pre-dementia, early stages of Alzheimer's disease. Mom desperately wanted me to live with them. I couldn't. My life was just getting back on track. They were set financially, so I helped her get a full-time nursing service. Of course, she didn't like them and she took over all of Dad's care on her own. She loved to rub it in and make me feel guilty. I wouldn't allow myself to get caught up in her little Venus Fly Trap. Dad knew I loved him. Mom started taking Vicodin on a regular basis to deal with her old injured hip. When I heard Dad got admitted to a nursing home, I half-wished she would join him.

I slept in my childhood bed, staring at the walls of pictures of friends I no longer had. In my mind, they had been replaced with degrees and accolades until my hospital stay. Mom must have changed it all around when she knew I'd be coming here, so I wouldn't get upset. That made it worse. I woke up every hour until 6:00 a.m. The aroma of coffee made me go out to the kitchen.

"Sorry, did I wake you, dear?" Mom was seemingly unruffled from last night's conversation. All things were forgiven in the morning and never brought up again.

"No, I smelled the coffee," I said, stifling a yawn. I pulled my chair out and sat down at our long glass kitchen table. Mom sat on the other side, a football-field away. It was the perfect picture of our relationship.

"I'm making scrambled eggs. They'll be ready in a minute, just letting the frying pan heat up." Mom slid out from under her chair. She didn't wait for me to answer. "You want some orange juice?"

"Orange," I giggled. "Yes, please." It was the first time I felt good in the last forty-eight hours.

"What's so funny?" Mom, oblivious to what was going on in my life, paused, and then continued to make breakfast.

We ate in painful silence. When I finished, I rose and walked over toward her. I hugged her tightly and she grabbed me into her arms as well. We muffled our crying.

"I love you, Mom."

Sunday afternoon at the nursing home, Dad slept most of the time I was there. Mom dozed off too from exhaustion. I used her cell phone to call and check on Ginger, who would be ready to come home on Tuesday. More good news. Then, I tried to reach Matt. When he answered the phone, he sounded sluggish and hung over.

"Matt, how are you?" I paced around the third floor of the nursing home.

"Lindsey? I didn't recognize the number you were calling from."

"Yeah, my phone is still at the police station. I'm using Mom's while they're both sound asleep in my Dad's room," I said.

"How are they?"

"Tired, overwhelmed. We all are. Dad had a lot of difficulty remembering who I was at first. He thought I was his head Nurse Kelly and I was forced to listen to all of *his* daughter's crimes and punishments." I stopped and leaned my back against a wall, stretching.

"That had to be rough. I'm sorry," Matt said once again. It appeared to be the only thing he knew how to say to me anymore.

"Me too."

"How is your mom taking it?"

"She's not happy with me. She thinks you and I should be engaged right now. We had a bang up, drag down fight last night. I confronted her. I wanted to know why she never came to see me in the hospital, you know, after it all happened."

"Jesus," he whispered.

"You sound tired. Were you up all night drinking with those guys at work?" All at once I got annoyed.

"Yeah, my head is killing me."

"I guess that means you won't be dropping by for a visit?" I purposely dawdled, turning in circles in my spinning skirt with low heel-shoes on, already knowing his answer.

"Oh, babe. If you had said you wanted me to stop by today, I wouldn't have partied so late. You told me you wanted to be alone, remember?"

I wasn't capable of putting two thoughts together right now. Had I ignored him? I didn't care at this point. What mattered was he didn't make me a priority after the hellish week I'd gone through. Business as usual. Gazing in my Dad's window, Mom's chin rested on her chest, sound asleep. Dad's eyes poked down the hall staring at me. His eyebrows crinkled and his mouth muttered something I couldn't hear.

"I have to go, Matt, get some rest. I'll be home later tonight." Worrying Dad had had another bad spell, I ran to his room. He looked at me like it was the first time he'd ever seen me. I stood in the doorway.

"Do I know you?" he whispered.

"Sometimes," I said honestly.

Dad's eyes vacillated between Mom, still sleeping, and me at his door. He placed his three middle fingers to his lips and blew me a kiss.

"Go, live your life. You don't belong here with us two old cronies." Water filled my eyes as I cried and blew him back a kiss. He snatched it up like a football player going for a long pass.

"I'll see you soon." Content I had done all I could, I went home. Time to heed his advice. Start living my life, do what I needed to do to be happy. I'd be back there at the nursing home one day soon enough.

I had let go of my past and felt the weight of the world drop off my shoulders.

# 17

# Tea for Two

I slept soundly for once. My body caved from pure mental and physical exhaustion. I awoke to silence. There was nothing stirring in the apartment, no boyfriend craving sex, no purring furry ball wanting a bowl of milk. It was just me in shadows of darkness which filled the apartment from the black sky with a crescent moon. Apparently, I had slept for two whole days. All I remember was calling about Ginger and making sure Dad was okay. The rest of the time I'd spent curled up reading or watching a decent movie. Carol left a message, checking in. Monday rolled around in no time.

Ginger would be coming home tomorrow. I made up my mind to break up with Matt. I was even happy to pay a visit a.s.a.p. to Sharon so she'd know how much I'd grown over this past week. I no longer desired a vacation or a lighter load of clients. Send me every kind of insanity you could muster. It was time to make Dad proud. I dressed in my best grey business attire, which consisted of a creamy white top, grey jacket with matching skirt. Since it was still cold out, I included white pantyhose with my long boots. My hair was up, jewelry was on, time to live my life and do what I do best.

Looking refined in his uniform and newly trimmed beard, Ben greeted me by opening the building door. I'd never been so happy to see someone in my entire life.

"You're here bright and early," he said jovially.

"Yes, I am," I added, "Well, someone has to be the one to tell you discreetly, you have chocolate icing smudged on your chin." I chuckled while licking my finger to wipe it off his face. He never made a move to stop me, just grinned toward the ceiling.

"Did you have a good weekend?" he asked.

"Let's say, I learned more in the last forty-eight hours than I had in weeks."

"Good! Well, you look...great," he stumbled for the right words. I provided a warm smile back to him, which made him blush.

"See you at lunch?"

"Sure, oh, Ms. CarMichael, not to dampen the mood, but did you by any chance make two appointments for the same time today?"

My mouth gaped. "I don't think so. Who signed in?" Reaching for the notepad spreadsheet, there indeed were Carrie Warner and Milo Cooper both signed in. "I feel like such an idiot!" I yelled, slapping my forehead with my free hand.

"Don't you go blaming yourself now," Ben pleaded. "You had one hell of a week. I don't know how you got through it all." He patted me on the back and then rested his hand there for a second. The hair on my arms stood on end.

"Okay, I won't." Smiling at Ben, I suddenly thought of an idea for the situation. "Thanks, Ben."

Scurrying down the hall to my waiting room, I took a deep breath and decided to go for broke. The two most innocent clients I worked with had a common denominator. I opened the door with my best apologetic face. Both Carrie and Milo sat in the room. Milo was tapping his hand on his leg as if drumming a song. Carrie was an ice figure, whose skeleton frame looked like it would crack any minute into a million pieces.

"Carrie, Milo, I'm so sorry. Please forgive me, I think I've made a terrible mistake. I'll be right back." Leaving the room and two of the most secluded people I knew, I wanted to see what would happen. I threw my purse and jacket on the desk. Then I slipped down on the wall closest to the waiting room to listen. Nothing. Five minutes went by, so I placed my ear on the wall, trying desperately to hear them. It was Milo who broke the silence.

"I wonder what she's doing in there? She must have really fucked up...er...I mean messed up. You know?"

"Yeah, she never took this long before with me," Carrie replied softly.

*Thank God, it's working,* I thought.

"So, what are you in here for?" Milo laughed. Thankfully Carrie joined in. I heard a cautious giggle escaping her.

"It does feel a little like a prison sentence, huh? Come to this place, share what you don't want to share or you'll be in *big* trouble," Carrie said.

Amazed that they were connecting, I let them continue, my ear still glued to the wall. Just in case I needed to bolt out and interrupt them, but so far, my plan was working.

"No shit! I was ordered to attend these sessions by my wife," Milo continued.

"Your wife?" Carrie sounded puzzled.

"Oh, yeah, we've never met. I'm Milo, an unhappily married man with no self-esteem. Nice to meet you." I heard him rise out of his seat as the chair squeaked.

*God, I needed a video camera in there.*

"Wow, I've never met a man who was so open and honest about being unhappy." Carrie's voice strengthened.

"I'm used to talking about it now. That wasn't always the case when I first started." Milo tried to sound nonchalant.

"Well, I hope you find happiness. I mean something substantial. Someone who brightens your day and makes you feel good to be alive, that's what I want."

I raised my hand and bit my thumbnail, smiling at my little group therapy going on without me.

"There's no reason you can't have what you want. I mean look at you, you're young and smart." He flattered Carrie. "In fact, why are you even here? If you don't mind me prying?" Milo, forever the gentleman, he deserved someone sweet like Carrie.

"No, I don't mind. After all, you shared your story. I should reciprocate." Carrie sounded bold.

"Reciprocate? That's a fancy word. What do you do?"

"I'm a teacher, or I was a teacher until I got sick." I heard a big exhale from Carrie. "I have an eating disorder. Food has always been a challenge for me. So, I too have issues to work on."

A silence between my two clients made me nervous and tense. I turned and got ready to open the door. Then stopped.

"I don't know much about eating disorders, maybe you're just insecure or some bad things happened to you. But, I think you should be proud and bravely hold your head up. You're stronger than you think," Milo said.

I kissed the inside of my office door when I heard him say this.

"That's very sweet of you. Thank you, Milo." Carrie's voice went soft. Time to intervene. I opened the waiting room door and both Carrie and Milo were smiling from ear to ear.

"Since I messed up both of your sessions, what do you say about going on a field trip?" I chirped, with arms flapping.

"What kind of trip?" Carrie asked.

"How about we have breakfast at Denny's? It will be my treat."

"Sounds good to me," Milo giggled.

Carrie lingered for a while. Milo picked up on why.

"Are you worried about eating with me? Because, I don't have to go if it makes you uncomfortable," he offered.

"No, I want you to come. Yes, let's do this," she said, turning toward me.

"Let me grab my purse and we're off!"

Smirking at Ben, I told him we were all going out for breakfast and I'd be back in an hour. We drove in our own cars. I wanted them both to have a way out if they became too anxious about the situation. Milo was used to being much more social than Carrie. However, Carrie was smarter than him and could see through all his bullshit. As long as she felt safe and in control, I had high hopes they'd become friends.

It was a little awkward at first, but the hard part was over. They knew each other's issues, which initiated honest conversations about their past. Carrie stared deep in thought when her pancakes arrived.

"Anything you want to talk about, Carrie?" I asked.

She shook her head and glanced up at Milo and me.

"No, not a thing. I am officially hungry." Carrie poured syrup and cut a huge slice, mixing it with strawberries, and ate the whole thing.

"Good choice," Milo said, doing the same.

"Can we do this every session?" Carrie asked as we laughed at our own goofiness.

"No, but this one is on the house, as I said. And I need to get back to work."

"No!" they said in unison.

"Yes, it's time. Carrie, I'll see you at 10:00 a.m. on Wednesday and Milo at 2:00 p.m. Sound good?"

Both nodded while still eating their food. They were happy. Imagine that? I had pulled it off.

"Be good, you two." My voice had a hint of sarcasm.

Back in my office, I called to check on Ginger. All was set for her going home tomorrow. I placed a call to Carol, who didn't have time to chat due to a double shift, but had loads to tell me about my vet. She agreed to meet me when I took Ginger home. No calls from Matt and I didn't care. I decided to call the police station and see if they had fixed my cell phone yet.

Officer Ted answered and said they had retrieved most of my files, but it would be another day for the pictures. So, I hung up and kicked off my tight boots. My feet needed a rest. Unfortunately, it was short-lived. The honorable Dr. Sharon Hingley phoned and requested my presence. This time I made her wait, just to piss her off. When I walked down to her office, I took my time and enjoyed the weather, the cool air gradually breezed by me, blowing though my hair. I was coming alive again, the old me no longer tainted from my past. I saw beauty in everything. The trees, the buildings, even my elevator ride to the top floor had a tremendous view. It brought tears to my eyes to think how numb and angry I'd been all this time.

When I opened the waiting room door to Sharon's office, I got the surprise of my life. Sharon had been waiting for *me*. I couldn't help but laugh at her appearance. Her arms were crossed and the left foot tapping. I felt as if I was twelve years old again and sent to detention for sticking out my tongue at little Stevie.

"What the hell did you do?" she clamored.

"Hello, Sharon, it's good to see you too." I refused to take the bait.

"Don't be coy with me, Lindsey. Is it true?"

"Is what true? Do you know how much has gone on this past week?"

"Milo and Carrie, did you take them out for breakfast?" Sharon charged into her office, demanding that I follow her with an arm motion. She nicely slammed the door after me. I swung around from the bang it made. I couldn't believe she was this upset.

"Yes, it's true. Is going out to Denny's now considered a crime?" I chuckled at the ridiculousness of the situation.

"This is not funny, Lindsey. Really, the audacity of it! You know damn well if you are going to conduct any sort of group therapy, you need another counselor present." Sharon pushed her chair against the wall and crossed her arms again acrimoniously. I decided to play it safe and concede. The last thing I needed was to be placed in front of the state board again.

"What if they start dating? What if they have sex? Or God forbid Milo says something that sets Carrie back to starving herself!" she said.

"No, it's not like that. You should have seen them. They were quite supportive of each other. Milo treated her with respect and Carrie downed two pancakes!"

Sharon ruminated over what I said, swiveling her black leather chair around which matched the dark pant suit she was wearing.

"All right, I'll give you a pass this time, but just this once. You hear me?"

"Yes, yes," I nodded, placating her.

"If they need any other group therapy, they can join my group on Thursday nights. And, remember you have that new case today, Kevin Marshal. Drop me an email after the session."

# 18

# Kevin Marshal

Monday January 13th, 2014, First Session
1:00p.m.

When I returned to my waiting room, a woman dressed in a blue navy dress, a man with a business suit and striped tie, and teenage boy wearing a black jean-jacket with a white-cross t-shirt underneath, sat in the room. My new patient with his parents had arrived and they smiled when I said hello. They were busy filling out the insurance form and details of what made them seek out therapy.

. "I need a minute and I'll be right out to see you," I told them, passing by. Kevin smiled at me. His buzz-cut, dark hair matched his outfit.

I gave them a few minutes while I made sure the room looked comfortable for three people. Pulling out the case of my new referral from the lovely Dr. Hingley, I started to read over it. Kevin Marshal, sixteen, would be attending with his parents, mother Abby and father Richard. Checking my lipstick and hair in the mirror, I opened the door to greet them.

"I'm so sorry," I apologized, "I've been running late all day."

"It's okay, dear," said the mother, "here, I filled out your form with our insurance information."

"I think we're a bit early anyway," said the father, nodding for approval. They all agreed with him by nodding, while entering the room.

I placed the coffee on my desk and read over the referral Sharon had given me. Knowing that all three of them were in attendance was a good sign. Therapy was best when family members were involved, obviously when there was a teenager at the core of the issue.

"Okay, I've read over your referral," I said, glancing at each of them with pleasantries and handshakes. "Sit wherever you want." Mom and Kevin took the couch as Dad plopped down on the chair.

"So, Abby is your name, and you are a—"

"Secretary for a law firm," she filled in the blank.

"And Richard?" I inquired.

"He is a car salesman," Abby answered for him. Richard nodded and looked at me. Someone didn't want to be here, I thought.

"Then, you must be Kevin," I said.

"I must be," Kevin smiled, showing neatly aligned bleached teeth at me. I assumed Abby and Kevin wanted the therapy, Richard was just for show. The proverbial "I'm not the one with the problem, it's them—fix them, please". The onion started to peel as it always did.

"So, what brings all of you here today?" I began.

"Frankly, Abby and I are worried about Kevin." Richard spoke, surprising me and Abby. Her head jerked back, looking toward her husband. Kevin gave a dismissive nod.

"What are you worried about with Kevin?" I asked Richard.

He leaned in his chair and sucked in his breath, with agitated wrinkles around his green eyes. "My boy skips school, smokes pot, been arrested for fighting, has no friends, right?" He directed his question to Kevin.

Kevin stared blankly without emotion and leaned back.

"Hell, I'd be happy if I caught the boy sleeping in our bed with a girl, for Christ-sake!"

"Richard!" Abby yelled in shock.

Richard sat back and crossed his legs. He had said what he'd come here to say. Richard looked satisfied.

Abby, embarrassed.

Kevin looked bored, as if he had heard this all before.

I paused to allow the dust to settle. This skill didn't always work with one-on-one sessions, but it was a goldmine for families. It allowed me to see who spoke first. Whoever did had the most skin in the game and wanted the therapy to be successful. (Hint: it wasn't usually the patient.)

"Is nobody going to say anything?" Abby asked, her voice sounding desperately shaky.

Richard looked frustrated. He crossed his legs in the opposite direction. Kevin sprawled his arms over the back of the couch.

"I will suggest something," I volunteered.

"Please do," Abby begged.

"Why don't Kevin and I spend the rest of the session talking, then I'll bring you both in at the end. Sound good?"

Abby's face relaxed. Richard jumped out of his seat as if it had been on fire.

"I have another idea," Richard interjected.

"What's that?" I moved up from my chair.

"I've been up since five this morning and I would like to go home now. It's one o'clock and I haven't had a whole afternoon off for so long. You can have your entire session with Kevin. Abby, let's get out of here and leave them to it."

"Richard, you promised me you would do family sessions," Abby chided.

"I will. But that Dr. Sharon, whatshername, said we'd have to do it a few times a month. And we just did one with her, so, next week will be a family session, okay?"

A second of silence filled the room. Richard placed his hand out toward Abby and lifted her up. Abby turned toward me.

"Okay, we'll see you next week then, Ms. CarMichael. I'm sorry about this, but when Richard makes up his mind. You know how it is," she said.

Richard stood in the waiting room looking back for Abby. I tried to reassure her.

"Therapy is a process. It takes time. Kevin and I will be all right, won't we, Kevin?" He forced a smile and looked happy to get rid of his parents.

"Yeah, we'll be fine, Mom. See you later."

"I'll call you when we're finished," I said to Abby.

"We live right around the corner!" Richard yelled from the waiting room. His tone became challenging. "The boy has legs, doesn't he?"

"Yes, Dad. Don't worry about me. I can walk home on my own," Kevin hollered.

I walked Abby out and closed the door to the waiting room. Returning to my chair, I heard Kevin say, "Alone at last."

"True, very true," I said. "You like to be alone, don't you?"

"Yes." Kevin rubbed his hands down the side of his jeans. "Wouldn't you if you had to put up with all that commotion in your own home?"

"My head went spinning there for a minute. Felt like a tiny tornado," I laughed out loud.

"So, what do you think doc? Am I crazy?"

"I think you're a teenager who has trouble controlling his anger. It's not the worst thing in the world. But, you do need therapy to learn how to get along better with your parents." I laughed. My job was to make the connection fast, or this family would be finished. I appeased him.

"Right?" Kevin laughed hysterically, "They're so gullible."

"Yes, but they did have some valid points, don't you think?" I asked.

"Sure, but it's my life. Why can't I live the way I want to?" Kevin said sternly. The glint of rage appeared ever so quickly.

"Your life and how you live it affects everyone, specifically your mom and dad," I said steadily.

"You're talking about when I act out and that started a few months ago. I got jumped in the locker room at school. I did what I was supposed to do and kept my mouth shut for a little while." Kevin took a deep breath. "But, they wouldn't leave me alone. So, I'm done trying to be what they think I should be."

"Do your parents know about this?" I said.

"Yeah, it was my dad who told me to keep my mouth shut. The asshole. I'll bet you fifty bucks he's home by now on his tenth cigarette."

"That's not okay," I said bluntly.

"He said that things would get worse for me if I told the school principal. So, I kept quiet."

I went to call his parents. "We all need to talk about this."

"No, don't get them," Kevin pleaded.

"Why not?"

"I'm going to take care of it."

"How?" I asked.

Kevin's eyes twinkled like the sun bouncing off an iced cube. "I'll tell you. But, you have to promise to keep it a secret."

I moved in my seat. "You know I can't make promises like that, Kevin," I assured him. "If you're planning on hurting anyone or yourself, I have to report it." My stomach churned. I didn't like where the conversation was going.

"You're my therapist. You have to keep secrets." He moved to the edge of his seat, a gesture of intimidation.

"What are you planning?" I asked, eyeing my panic button under my desk. Ben and the boys would be here in a jiffy once I pushed it.

"I'm going to kill them all," he said in a flat tone.

Reaching below with my hand, I found the panic button. My fingernails scaled the edges of the device. Being subtle was lost; Kevin eyed me closely as I reached quickly to press it.

"How is Ginger doing?" he asked.

I froze. Goosebumps covered my arms. Chills rushed up my spine.

"Let me see your hands, stand up," Kevin blurted out.

I sat back in my chair and surrendered. There still would be time to alert the police. So, I chose to keep him talking. I'd have to catch him off guard. I rose and stood still.

"You're the one who hurt my cat?" I spoke softly.

"Yes, sorry, but it had to happen. I had to get your attention, so you'd know I meant business when I came here tonight."

"That was a week ago. How did you—"

"I did my research. You don't think I'd tell just anyone my secrets, do you? Especially what I'm planning and I knew you'd have to report me, because that's what you guys do."

"Yes, we do. What are you planning?" My voice quivered expectantly.

"I have guns, I have ammo and...now, I have you." He showed no emotion.

My lips tightened. Every muscle felt paralyzed.

"What do you mean you have me?" I asked.

"You're going to go down in the history books as the therapist who helped kill teenagers in a mass school shooting."

My vocal chords made no sound. I swallowed hard, trying to force a scream.

"There is a soccer practice going on right now. It's a sport I use to play, until those assholes started harassing me. I have the bomb all set to go off anytime I want. See?" Kevin opened his jacket and proudly displayed the bomb wrapped around the mid-section of his body.

"Oh God!" I cried.

"Please don't get upset." Kevin approached and knelt down in front of me. "I'm not going to hurt you as long as you do what I say." He smoothly pulled a semi-automatic from the back of his shirt.

"What do you want?" I closed my eyes.

"Let's go to your house. I know where you live. God, that sounds so corny to say out loud!" He chuckled. Then he composed himself. "I also know where Matt lives, where Ben lives and I know where Carol lives. I even know where that bitch Dr. Sharon Hingley resides."

"You'll never get away with this," I said defiantly.

"Oh, don't worry about me. You've had such a rough week, how is your dad doing at the Coral Bay Nursing Home, room 318 is it?"

I gasped.

"Let's go for a drive. You hungry? I hear Denny's makes some decent pancakes."

"We're taking my car?" I couldn't feel my body.

"Yes, I'm all yours for the next few hours. Let's have some fun. Come on, move nice and slow," he ordered me.

"I can't, my legs feel like rubber bands." I cringed with each step. My breathing quickened, which made each muscle hurt.

"You'll feel better once we get past the guards, when you get to see lover boy."

*Please God, let Ben be at his desk.*

As Kevin and I rounded the corner I saw Ben sitting at his desk, feet up. One of his fellow officers (whose name escaped me) joked around with him. I gagged a loud cough to get their attention. It worked. However, Kevin brandished a side firearm from under his pants and introduced it to my ribcage, hidden from view. My breathing quickened. Sweat emerged from under my arms and forehead. Ben did a quick double take when he saw me. He stood and walked in our direction.

"Nice and easy, I don't want to have to hurt him," Kevin mumbled with a smile. I returned the smile which made Ben's facial muscles relax.

"All done for the day?" Ben asked, moving closer.

"Yeah, Matt is waiting for me." This statement caused the reaction I wanted from Ben, jealousy. It threw him off guard, literally. He no longer focused on Kevin, but on the fact I had a boyfriend—and Ben had kissed me recently. I figured distraction was the only way to save him. Otherwise, there would be bloodshed before we left the building.

"See you guys tomorrow?" I said, as Kevin jammed the gun harder. I glanced straight ahead and Kevin eased up.

"Have a good one," Ben said as Kevin and I walked out of the building toward my car.

# 19

# Soccer Practice

"You did very well. You held your cool in there. Good thing too, that cop was giving me the evil eye. You know he has a boner for you, right?" Kevin smirked as he got in the passenger seat of my car.

Getting in next to him, I said nothing. I had to start thinking ahead. What was his game plan? How could I counter it? I noticed out of the corner of my eye Kevin was peering at me.

"What are we doing?" I whispered.

"First, you start the car and then we go to my school. Soccer practice is about to begin, and I would just hate to miss this session. The team is counting on me to pull them through, you know," Kevin said, breaking out in laughter at his own sarcasm.

"What if I refuse to go?" I asked, as timidly as I could.

"Then, I kill you now and toss you in the back seat. Drive over and kill your parents at the rest home. Gun down Matt after he gets off work, the same with Carol and my parents. Because, I figured I'll need a few hours' sleep. Then I blow up the school tomorrow instead. Your choice." Kevin reached for his gun and aimed it at my head. I trembled uncontrollably. Then I slowly reached up at the gun and lowered it.

"I'll stay with you the whole time," I said. The car started right up and I backed out of my parking place. Kevin jumped up and down like a little boy, giggling with joy.

"The wonderful therapist Lindsey CarMichael will be in attendance at *my* greatest achievement!" He chuckled nefariously some more while I stared at the road. After about five minutes, the weight of what he was about to do became palpable inside the car.

"I know what happened to you, you know?" he said.

"What do you mean?" I spun my head in his direction.

"The case you had, the young girl named Angel. How she died from the kid who was abusing her. It made you go crazy, didn't it?"

"For a while, yes. I blamed myself. The State blamed me, my mom blamed me and all I wanted was to die."

"That had to be rough...I know how that feels," Kevin said with a single nod of his head. "Hey, but good work getting Carrie Warner and Milo Cooper together," Kevin said, changing the subject.

"What do you mean, together?" I questioned.

"Last time I checked was right before our session. The two of them were fucking like rabbits. Seems to me like it was the perfect medicine for both of them. Milo deserved it after dealing with that controlling bitch of a wife and Carrie just needed to feel desirable again. I bet they end up getting married."

"It's not as simple as that, Kevin. They both have many issues to work out and—"

I caught myself mid-thought. Why the hell was I having this conversation?

"You don't want to talk about it anymore?" he said.

"No."

"In case you make it out of here in one piece, huh?"

I didn't answer him. My hands began to tremble.

"Turn right at the next corner. We're going to the stadium parking lot in back of the high school." I didn't need to have my windows down to hear the roar of the teenage players counting as they warmed up.

"Where do I park?" I asked, staring at the stadium benches full of soccer parents and other students watching.

"There," Kevin pointed, "right up front."

I did as I was told. Voices and whistles distracted me. I felt my hands go clammy.

"Can I ask you a question? Why did you pick me?" I stalled, waiting for a miracle.

Kevin grinned maliciously, then straightened his lips. He looked out over the stadium field where the boys had started to run laps around the track. I didn't know if he was waiting for more people to arrive or simply relishing the experience.

"Well, first off, I liked the history you've experienced, like I mentioned. But, when I found out you were a prodigy in the field—one of the youngest students ever to get published, the deed was done. Specifically, when I found out the topic you chose. Of course you remember the thesis, don't you?"

"National Report studies indicate that the age of highest risk for the initiation of serious violent behavior is age sixteen," I said, tears swelling my vision.

Kevin yanked his gun out of the way so he could shove his face close to mine. "But, honestly, you were just in the right place at the right time—like you are now." He leaned back and adjusted his clothes. Unzipping the jacket that revealed four strapped-on pipe bombs to his abdomen, Kevin pulled out a computerized button. He clicked it and the front of his vest flashed green. "Ready?"

"No, no, no, please, Kevin. You still can come back from this. I won't tell anyone what you did. I promise. Look, there are children out there. Why don't I pay for self-defense lessons and teach you to fight? Then, you beat the shit out of those bullies." My voice had turned to sobs. I choked in between sentences.

"You don't understand. Once you get to this point in your life, there's no going back, not ever. What? Did you think I would change my mind and go be in therapy with you, like just another patient? That's nuts."

He looked inside his jacket. Every pocket was filled to the top with ammo. He grabbed the gun he had kidnapped me with and proffered it in my direction.

"There were never any bullets. I just needed it for show—like I need you now for show. Let's go. It's time. Coach is gathering them all in a circle, looks like they're sitting down."

Peering out the window, I could see Kevin was right. He snapped the side door open and smoothly moved his wired body to the ground, standing upright.

"Kevin, I can't do this," I cried inside the car. My feet weighed like bricks. Inertia had its hold on me.

For a second, his eyebrows knitted together in thought. Then a flash of white teeth smeared across his face.

"If you don't get out of the car right now, I will kill everyone you love." Sweat dripped down my back, heat filled my cheeks, fluctuating with the cool air of the afternoon. *I'm going to die today,* I thought. My side door opened as Kevin walked over to greet me. I glanced up at him and saw the hazy sky, the sun blocked by his head.

"What do I do now?"

"Hide the gun in your pants until I say 'Draw'. Then you aim it at the crowd." Kevin spoke to me like I was a child. He yanked me out of the car and we began the slow death march toward the stadium. My mind left my body. I couldn't think. Kids were playing with their parents. Cheerleaders practiced their routines—dancing around. I had a vision of Angel being shot, over and over.

As we moved within reach of the stadium, people's heads turned. I didn't understand what was happening. Kevin's face turned to mine.

"DRAW!" he yelled, running as he dragged me with him. He placed me on the back end of the circle of soccer kids who were sitting down. I was parallel to the coaches and stadium bleachers. Kevin walked to the far end of the field so he had full view.

"I said DRAW!" he shouted again. I retrieved my gun, aiming it at the crowd. Tears splashed down to my chest. Kevin pulled out his semi-automatic rifle and pointed it at the boys, one boy in particular.

"Nobody fucking move." Kevin took charge. He grinned as he sucked in all the power he'd now possess. The grin diminished as he squatted down and aimed his weapon directly at his antagonist. "I hope you said your morning prayers, Alex, are you ready to meet your maker?" The screaming started and people tried to run away or grabbed hold of each other in shock. Kevin fired the gun up in the air. The sound of thundering explosions each time the gun fired was heard. It resembled the grand finale of a fireworks display. However this version had people screaming for their lives. Being in close proximity to the bleachers made the echoing effect worse.

Kevin told them to lie down on the field. He unzipped his jacket so they could see the bomb.

"The rules are simple, you run, my lovely therapist shoots you and then I blow everyone up," he said. Sounds of sobbing mixed with tiny screams and prayers could be heard.

If I was to survive this, I had to follow the rules Kevin had set out and acclimate myself to them. I wanted to save as many people as possible. Judging him by his demeanor, he wanted this to last as long as it could. I decided that was his weak spot, gloating. Alex drew most of his attention. He'd shoot him first. He must have been the bully ring-master who tortured Kevin. A sudden movement came from the left corner of my vision.

One of the coaches had stepped in front of a little girl. Quickly, the coach tugged at his back jeans. He held a gun and shot at Kevin, but missed. Kevin returned fire and hit. The coach went down as blood splattered from his stomach. Sirens could be heard in the background. A moment of silence was then followed by Kevin screaming as if a werewolf. His mental snap was complete.

"Yeah, baby!" Kevin ran toward the coach as a few people dove under the steel bleachers to take cover. "Anyone else want to mess with me, motherfuckers? This party has officially begun." He shot more bullets up in the air and then terrified all of us by waving the little magic button in his hand that would detonate his bomb. He then headed for Alex who was crouched down with hands over his head. I tried to distract him. Maybe the police would get here in time. But what then?

"Kevin, what are you doing? Really? You allowed that little piece of shit bully you!" I said, pointing at Alex.

Kevin looked at me in disbelief. As if I had betrayed him by mentioning all of his dirty little secrets out into the world. His expression went from rage—wide eyed—to complete calm, face relaxed. He tore over to me, dragging the hysterical Alex on hands and knees with him. Once he reached me, he placed a pistol in my hand.

"Just for that, I'll let you do the honors. Careful with the gun, that one is loaded. Kill Alex now or you die." Kevin backed away from me and aimed his semi-automatic at my head. The gun was so heavy.

"Please, Kevin, I'm so sorry," Alex begged.

"Shut the fuck up, you piece of shit. You die today," Kevin said and he nudged his head toward Alex. "Do it," he ordered, then opened the palm of his hand to show me the bomb detonator.

Sirens were getting closer.

"I can't," I said, sobbing.

"Yes, you can, just a gentle pull of the trigger."

"No, I won't do it." I collapsed on my knees and heard the police cars pull in every direction around the stadium.

"Do it now or I swear I'll blow us all up to kingdom come." Kevin jammed his gun at my head. A voice came over the loudspeaker.

"Put down your weapons and place your hands on your head," an officer said.

"He has a bomb strapped to his chest!" one of the coaches yelled. Kevin swiftly looked over to the coach—his eyes squinting, aiming. I couldn't let another person get hurt. I shot Kevin in the shoulder and tried to protect Alex by covering him with my body.

Kevin screamed and I heard two gunshots, and piercing bites of my flesh filled with fire in my back. I tasted blood and moaned from the searing pain. My chest filled up with fluid as breathing became taxing. My ear drums had been blown so I never heard the third shot. It came from where the police parked. One bullet shot at Kevin. It hit him straight in his head. His body collapsed next to mine. We were face to face. I watched as the life left his body.

The horror show had ended. People lined up with their hands over their heads and ran to safety. I forced myself to turn over on my side and let Alex crawl out unwounded.

"Thank you," he sobbed.

The pain of the bullets started to spread through my body. My right shoulder blade stung as if I was bitten by a thousand bees. I stopped moving for fear of losing blood.

The police circled around Kevin and me. I told them the bomb was still active and the switch was in his hand. Then I was placed on a stretcher. Shaking violently, I kept waiting for the bomb to go off. It never did.

In the hospital, I was told everyone survived but Kevin. The coach was released after a few days. Kevin's parents asked for my forgiveness, which I easily provided. He had made a video of his plan, but neither one of them had turned it on until they saw what was happening at the school from the local news.

# 20

# Recovery

When I came into the hospital, it was vital that the police were able to interview and debrief me. However, my spleen ruptured early on during an interview. I began to lose consciousness, all the while hearing the doctor and nurses prep me for surgery. Since I had been shot at close range, my blood loss was dramatic.

"We'll need to set up for a blood transfusion," the doctor told one of the nurses.

"Her blood pressure is dropping. Let's move, people."

While I was blacking out I saw a vision of Kevin still with his ominous grin.

***

"Honey, open your eyes. It's okay. You're safe now." Carol spoke tenderly. Many jumbled heads came into my blurry view: Matt, Carol, Ben, Mom and even Sharon—all of them smiling.

"Oh, God, am I dying?" The joke went over well, my family and friends all enjoyed it.

"No," Carol butted in, "unfortunately, you're going to make it. Bless your heart." She smiled and gave me a wink.

"How are you feeling, babe?" Matt said, as he came into view. He had a terrified expression, with his tongue half out and a wrinkled forehead. This was new territory for him and I sort of felt bad that he was going through it with no support.

"Like I've been shot two times," I replied, taking his hand.

"Welcome to the club," Ben added as he stood behind everyone, guarding the door.

"Do I get an official badge or something?" I joked with him.

"I'll see what I can do. But I think with all the media attention you're receiving, the mayor will give you the key to the city once you get out of here."

Mom waved off Ben with her hand as if she didn't want me to know something. She looked the worst out of everyone as she approached my side. Ben warmly smiled and moved out of the room, closing the door behind him. He stood his post there.

"My darling girl," Mom cried as she bent down to kiss me. "What kind of world are you living in? You shouldn't have patients like that boy." Mom pointed to the TV in the corner I hadn't noticed until then. "See what I mean!" Mom said.

The national news networks picked up the story. Kevin's face went to close up as they showed videos of the event from a courageous or stupid bystander. Another video displayed him at his house, recording all he was going to do. I turned away.

"I don't think we need to see this. Lins needs a break," Carol said, coming to my rescue, and turned it off.

"Thank you, my dear," I added.

Mom pouted. She didn't know what to do with herself. She claimed a tiny chair and sat listening.

"How is Dad doing, Mom?" I asked, trying to include her.

"He's the same. You know, in one minute and out to lunch the next. I never know which one he's going to be. I miss him so much." Mom began to cry, as did the rest of us. Carol gave her a tight hug and a kiss on the cheek.

Although I gazed up at Matt, my eyes tended to flicker past him to see Ben standing, protecting me.

"Well, Lindsey, what are you going to do for an encore?" Matt chortled.

"I think I'll run for President," I laughed with everyone until I felt a sudden tinge of pain.

"Easy, Lins, you've still have some healing to do." Carol nodded.

"Thank you, Nurse Ratchet," I moaned

"I think the painkillers are wearing off," Dr. Hingley added her two cents. I gawked at her.

"Just imagine all the fun things we will get to talk about later," I said. That made her smile.

"I'll be waiting. Now, time for my next session and I know you're in good hands here. Please call me soon," Dr. Hingley said, looking around the room. She affectionately squeezed my hand and left the room leaving Matt, Carol and Mom to take care of me.

"Oh, my God! How is Ginger?" I grabbed Carol's hand. She patted it with a mischievous smirk.

"She's doing wonderful. Don't you worry about her."

I laughed again, forgetting about the pain. "Are you or is my vet taking care of her?" I teased.

"Let's just say, she's getting the best care possible."

"Jesus," I said.

A long pregnant pause filled the room. The laughter had all been used up. Images of a twisted sixteen-year-old boy's face came flooding through my mind. We had been inches away from each other on the ground—a tiny hole right between his eyes. That stare would haunt me for the rest of my life.

"You look tired, babe," Matt said, kissing my hand.

"I am," I agreed.

"Let's go have dinner and let Lindsey sleep a little bit." Matt waved to Mom and Carol, who nodded.

"If it's okay, I think I'll go home and check on your father," Mom said.

"Sure, give him a kiss for me." Mom bent over and planted one on my head.

We all said our goodbyes. I watched as one after the other exited the room through the door Ben guarded. Matt even stopped and shook Ben's hand. They chatted a little but I couldn't hear them. Matt left. Ben looked at me and did a quick wave.

I drifted off to sleep. I dreamed of being in my car, driving through town. My first stop was the rest home Dad was living the remainder of his life in. Rain pounded my car windows, so I sat there a little while and left.

I drove by the factory plant where Matt worked. The night's rainy clouds lifted. A full moon rose. It shone its brilliant glow down on the parking lot. There, on the end row of parked cars was a beige Chrysler. My heart jumped through my throat. I tore out of my car.

"Matt! Matt! The car is here! Kevin is watching you!" I screamed until I collapsed on my knees. Warm fluid seeped through my shoulder and stomach. My hands reached under to find what was wrong. Pulling out two small objects, my hands reflected the moon's light with bloodstained bullets in each palm. "NO!" I cried, getting up and running back to my car.

The empty streets puzzled me. There wasn't a car in sight. The stores were empty. Still, I waited at each traffic light until it turned green. Night turned to day in an instant. I had to shade my eyes. Around the corner, I heard a cry. I braked quickly and got out. There, covered in sewage and blood with a stick poking out of her eye and singed fur, was a Bengal cat, my Ginger. Before I could reach her, a young black girl gallantly cradled Ginger up in her arms with a white blanket.

"I'll take her to the vet for you. Thank you for trying to save me. I'm not in pain anymore." Angel, my little guardian, smiled while she walked away.

Footsteps approached me from behind. I felt the edge of the semi-automatic gun at my back.

"Drive," Kevin sneered at me when I turned toward him. "Come on, the police will be here soon." Then, we were back at the stadium sitting in my car. I peered over to see Kevin's face. His head puffed up like a balloon that had exploded in the back. I still could smell the gunpowder from his body. When he faced me, I could see through his eyes all the way to the stadium from the back of his head being blown off.

"Do you feel better now, too?" I questioned.

"I don't feel anything, never have, never will."

"Interesting," I said, tending to my wounds.

"Can I ask you something? Why did you really want to be a therapist?"

"Because, I'm fucked up, all therapists are, most of them are crazier than the people they treat. Shh!" I placed my forefinger up to my lips. "Please don't tell anyone. It's an acquired skill, in order for you to get people to believe the truth about themselves, you have to master the art of lying."

I woke up with a jolt to the TV broadcasting Kevin's homemade video once more. Matt was sound asleep by my side. Ben continued his sentry duty.

*"A lot of people will get hurt today and I am not sorry for that. I didn't become this monster overnight, no one does. It takes years. Unless your parents suck, then it happens much faster.*

*I'll do my best to kill Alex and his gang. Then I'll die willingly. Sorry to Lindsey CarMichael, my therapist, I just wanted you to be there in case...you know, anyone needs psychological help. It's a terrible world we live in. I give us another hundred years or so, then poof. Glad I won't be there to witness it."*

Tears drained from my eyes. I reached over to Matt's hand that was resting on the bed. He rose and sat close to me, softly squeezing my good shoulder.

"Had a bad dream?" he said, wiping my face dry.

"Awful, so very awful," I sobbed too loud, and saw Ben look my way. Briefly smiling at him, I placed my head on top of Matt's chest—making my choice.

# 21

# Awards, Accolades and a Key

My father was right. I had become a famous therapist even if it was for merely one day. In a quiet and respectful ceremony, February 4th, 2014 became known in the city of West Palm Beach as Lindsey CarMichael's Day. I was given the key to the city, which didn't unlock anyone's door. Given its five and three-quarters inches in length, I'd imagine it worked on cages in the zoo, good for nothing.

People found me to be quite charming and said I displayed a courageous persona risking my life to save others. Mom and Dad were guests of honor and were able to sit on stage during the celebration. Matt and Sharon sat together in the front row, Carol right behind them. I would have loved to hear what they all chatted about. Matt looked nervous. Carol made outrageous facial expressions. I had to pinch myself to stop laughing.

After two hours of shaking everyone's hand and brunch at Carol's house, I collapsed in the guest bedroom with a healed one-eyed cat. Ginger and I hadn't been separated for a day since I came home from the hospital. We were both considered wounded in the field for righteousness, Dad declared. I accepted.

With this acceptance, it became clear as water that I needed help. I went to a meeting for PTSD survivors every day and saw Dr. Hingley, or Sharon as she subsequently allowed me to call her. The bitch.

Given the all clear for the second time in my career, I resumed my therapy sessions, but exclusively with my two clients. Carrie and Milo.

Both of them were amazed at my ordeal and wanted to spend more time asking me questions than working on their own issues. "My dear, I feel like you're distracting me so we won't have time to discuss you," I told her.

"Maybe, but you have to admit this was pretty hard to digest. I mean, you could have died!"

"I know," I said, rising to playfully hit her in the head with one of the stuffed animals.

Carrie laughed for a while and then became serious. "I can't believe I used to do the things I did to myself."

"You've come a long way, baby," I said in a funny expression. But it was true, she had. Her weighed was a hundred and five pounds. Her hair was cut shorter and her mom was helping her with dental work.

"I know, right? I have a job interview next week."

"Really? That's wonderful. What kind?" I asked.

"A substitute teacher, baby steps, you know. Mom is out of her mind happy." Carrie smiled.

"I'll bet. Congratulations!"

"Thanks, Milo is thrilled too," she whispered.

My mouth dropped open.

"I didn't realize you were seeing him."

"Yeah, it was after you almost died that we both realized life is short. He left his wife and we dated. Mom is in love with him. You know she just wants me out of the house."

"Not true," I said. "Would both Milo and you like to have couple sessions together? I think it would be a good idea as well as to continue on with individual sessions."

"Sure, he's outside in the waiting room." Carrie had changed before my eyes. I hoped they weren't moving too fast.

"Wow, you go get Milo as I make a quick phone call. Okay?

"Yeah, I'll be right back." Carrie jumped up and went out the door.

I called Sharon to see it she wanted to do something different with them, make sure my tracks were covered.

"Sharon, I have Carrie and Milo in my waiting room. They did indeed start dating."

"I told you that might happen." She rubbed it in.

"My point is, do you trust me enough? I feel ready for this," I said determined.

"Are you sure? Maybe all of this excitement is causing you to skew your judgment."

"I can do it, Sharon," I said.

"No, you can't. You're snapping at me—"

"Of course, because you're being ridiculous!"

"And now you're screaming, listen. Just make it a casual get together and say hello. Then come over to my office please. Goodbye." Sharon hung up. I seethed into the empty phone.

I straightened out my navy dress and took a deep breath. "Easy, Lindsey," I told myself. Then I opened the door to the waiting room.

"Hey, Ms. Superstar!" Milo bellowed.

"Hello, Milo, how are you?" I played down what he said.

"I'm just so happy, *we* are just so happy you're safe and sound," he said, throwing an arm around his new girlfriend.

"Thank you, please come in," I gestured with my arm.

Curling up on the sofa, the two lovebirds squeezed together, smiling at each other. It seemed like years had passed since Milo sat deflated in front of me—his shoulders slumped over. Now, he'd assumed a new personality as well. They were a match. I didn't understand how, but it worked.

"So, tell me what's been going on?" I smiled.

Each of them looked at one another to see who would speak first. They both did at once with a stumble. Bursting out with laughter at their nervous excitement, Carrie took the lead.

"Ever since that day last month when we went to Denny's, well, we've been inseparable. Right, honey?" Carrie looked for Milo's approval of the facts.

"You got it, honey." Milo nodded in my direction.

"And—what about your wife, Milo? Is it over?"

"Yes, I filed for divorce two weeks ago. I've never been happier. And I owe it all to you," he said.

"Me? Why's that?"

"It took me seeing you risk your life for someone else to realize that I was in a loveless marriage and wasting my time. Carrie and I began to hang out a lot after that day. We became friends first and then fell in love." Milo reached for Carrie's hand and they hugged each other intimately.

"Well, it's great to see you two so happy. And you need to both give yourselves a lot of credit. You've worked hard to get to a place in your life that you're able to be in a stable relationship."

"Thanks, I agree." Carrie planted a long kiss on Milo which made him blush.

"Remember, we still have more work to do, okay?" I cautioned them. I feared they were getting ahead of themselves. "Take things slow and I'll see you Carrie on Wednesday at ten o' clock and Milo on Thursday at one."

"Sounds good," Milo said. Carrie wrote out her check for the session and the two of them left.

I dashed out through the hallway, running by Ben who yelled, "Is there a problem?"

"No, I have a meeting with Dr. Hingley and I'm running late," I lied.

Once outside, I slowed my pace. Ever since the shooting, I'd made excuses to always be in a dreadful hurry to pass by Ben. We had several awkward conversations whenever we bumped into each other in the hall. I knew it hurt him when I chose to stay with Matt. So, I avoided his work station at all times.

My arms crossed as the evening air went from cool to cold. I thought what I would say to Sharon. My breathing increased every step I moved closer to her office. The gall of the woman to challenge me like that, really! She treated me as if I was a child. While I was the one who saved the city from being just another statistic by having a mass school shooting. All she had done was miss the signs of the young psychotic lad with a hidden agenda. She should be kissing my ass.

The electric doors flew open and I signed in. Going up in the elevator, I made meticulous plans on how I would ever so politely tell Sharon to go fuck herself. But, once the doors opened, I lost my nerve.

Sitting in her waiting room, eyes down, I had a flashback of my dream with Kevin. Sharon called my name and I didn't even hear her.

"Lindsey!" Sharon's feet stood before me. I glanced up in shock. Where had I gone?

"Didn't you hear me? I called your name twice."

"Yes, I heard you," another lie escaped. "I was deep in thought."

"Come inside and tell me what happened," Sharon ordered.

I rose and performed the Nazi salute while she turned her back. Of course, I started laughing silly but she ignored me and asked, "What is so funny?" Sharon went to her chair.

"Nothing. Just thought of a stupid joke." I shrugged my shoulders like I did whenever I became anxious.

"Are you okay?" Sharon's eyes were deadly serious. Petrified I would burst out laughing at her, I forced a cough and rose to get water from her cooler.

"Let me say this," my childish behavior under control, "Milo and Carrie have never looked or sounded better."

"That's wonderful to hear. My concern is with you. You became very terse with me when I confronted you on the phone."

"I'm very sorry. I truly apologize." *And lie number three has been noted, do I hear a lie number four?*

"Thank you, I appreciate that. Remember that a short fuse is a symptom of PTSD. You must think and act slowly."

"I will. And both Carrie and Milo are continuing on with their individual sessions."

"Good, do they want to pursue couple's therapy?"

"I don't know, but, given that Milo's wife was so against it, he might really be interested. I assumed you would like to handle their sessions and we could keep better tabs on them." I knew this was coming, so I beat Sharon to the punch.

"Wonderful attitude," she said. Feeling frisky, I decided to test my limits.

"Are there any other cases you could refer to me?"

"Really?"

"Yes, I think I can handle one more, don't you think? Something easy, like depression or addiction?"

"Take your pick." She pulled opened her desk drawer full of manila folders with names on them.

"Wow! Are there that many?" I asked, amazed that all those people were waiting for help.

"Yes, we got a huge number of requests for you personally after you became famous. I couldn't keep up with them."

"I know. They all think I can walk on water now, right?"

"That's one way of putting it." Sharon smiled. I closed my eyes and grabbed one folder, not knowing anything about the case.

"Wait, let me see it first, just to be sure." She reached out for me to hand it over.

I opened my mouth to complain, but then stopped short of saying anything.

Taking her time, flipping through its contents, I started to despise her once more. "Very well, a depressive addict, you got your wish. I'll call her and let you know when. Are you on your way home?"

"Yes, ma'am. Goodbye."

# 22

# My Breakup with Matt

Ginger and I had been curled up in bed watching TV. My one-eyed companion took a break from jumping on the window curtains to test her strength. I was feeling rejuvenated from having a few days off. Sharon phoned about my new client and scheduled the appointment. Thunder began cracking as looming clouds rolled toward my apartment. Neither one of us enjoyed the lightning strikes, so we hovered together steadily under my blanket. I heard the front door squeak open as a key twisted it. My body jerked up as did Ginger's ears.

"Matt, is that you?" I attempted not to sound afraid even though my heartbeat was racing. His sturdy frame entered through the door.

"Man alive, I just got soaked!" He laughed it off while shaking his head.

"Jesus Christ, Matt! Take your fucking shoes off! You're tracking mud all over the place," I hollered.

"It's nice to see you too, sweetheart." His voice was sarcastic and rough, as if he'd just finished smoking his usual limit of two packs of cigarettes.

"You know how hard it is for me to keep this place clean!"

"I know, I know. Me and my dirty shoes and smelly shirt drive you nuts," he said in a huff.

"A little heads up would have been nice too. I didn't know you were coming over. Why didn't you call?" I shot him a glance.

Matt stopped dead in his tracks and looked at me with a frustrated frown. He placed his hands by his side and twisted his palms toward me. Playing the martyr card as water continued to drip off his clothes.

"I wasn't aware that I had to call. What the hell is wrong with you tonight?" he asked, rolling his eyes.

Throwing my legs across the bed, unsettling Ginger who let out a wince of disapproval, I stood up and tied my robe in a bow. I was ready for a fight whether or not Matt deserved one. We dawdled in the hall for a second. Neither of us said a word. Who would draw first blood? Breaking the inertia, I walked over to him with my fists clenched. I truly felt like I was going to hit him. What stopped me was his smell. A strong mixture of sweat and cigarettes that made me gag.

"Holy shit, Matt!" I covered my mouth and nose with my hand. My whole face wrinkled as I turned away from him.

"You looked like you were going to hit me," he said lowering his voice to a whisper. His face turned white.

"What? No, I wasn't," I said coughing. "Please go take a shower and I'll toss your stuff in the washer." I made my best sympathetic face trying to hide the fury underneath my skin. We were going to have angry sex tonight or none at all.

"Sure thing, sweetie," he said with a cautious gaze in my direction. I cringed at his tone while bending over. Matt pushed off his shoes with his toes. He then handed me his filthy socks and shirt.

"What about your pants?" I asked.

"Hold on, hold on. God, you're impatient tonight." He then reached for his wallet and cell phone, placing them on the nightstand. Next I was inundated with his jeans and underwear—complete with skid-marks.

"Nice," I said, showing him the stain. He refused to comment and laughed instead.

"I'll be in the shower if that's okay with you," he said while walking away, not caring to look back.

Ginger purred at my feet as I stood there filled with rage. I walked through the kitchen until I reached the laundry room. My cat followed me and took a piss in her box. A quick glance and I told her, "You and Matt have a lot in common." She purred as if she was questioning me. "You both get to shit in my house and I look the other way." I held up Matt's clothes and took a good whiff. *What the hell was that smell?* Perfume. And not mine.

I froze there while the washer filled with water. The sudden shake coming from inside the machine jolted me out of my shock. I turned the handle to 'Machine Wash Hot' and pushed his clothes in until I felt my skin scorching. I forced my arms in the steaming water as long as I could. Robotically, I lifted my arms up. I could see large crimson blisters forming. Scorching pain followed. Gazing at Ginger, I said, "Remember that a short fuse is a symptom of PTSD. You must think and act slowly." She ran out of the room.

I moved in slow motion out to the kitchen and opened the fridge. The shiny yellow stick of butter called my name. I grabbed it and pretended it was soap. Each forearm was fully slathered with the grease. And all I could think about was popcorn.

"Something smells good," Matt said as he entered the room with a towel wrapped around him.

"Does it? It must be the butter I had to use on my arms." I showed him the red blotches.

"Shit! What did you do, babe?" He flinched back a step.

"What did I do? I did nothing, the water was too hot and your clothes splashed on me."

"Oh God, they look real bad, honey. Should we go to the ER?"

"No, I'll live. Butter and cool water is the best remedy."

Matt moved closer to me and tried to help with the smearing of butter. He kissed my cheek and neck. Pulling away, I went back to the fridge.

"I'm so sorry, babe. Is there anything I can do?" he asked, moving in my direction.

"Who is she?" I said, staring at him straight in the eyes.

Matt's face went gray. He shook his head as if confused. As he raised his hand to push his hair back, I enjoyed watching his trepidation. I enjoyed him trying to find the correct words to use. *Choose wisely, babe.*

"I don't know what to say." The bastard admitted it.

I moved inches toward his face. "I said. Who is she?"

"You don't know her. I met her about a month ago. It was one time."

"About a month ago, really? Was it that night I called you and you said you had to take on a double shift at work?" Spittle gathered on the edges of my mouth. I stood there in shock.

Matt bowed his head lower. He nodded yes. At that exact instant, my knee jerked up and smacked him in the balls. *Talk about your knee jerk reaction!* He toppled over, not making a sound as the green towel around his waist fell to the floor. I stared straight ahead. It would have ended there and then. However, Matt had the audacity to reach over with his hands and touch my bare feet. Groaning with gurgling sounds, he pleaded, "Honey, please help me."

I allowed him to wallow for a second. As my eyes peered down at him crying silently in pain, I met his gaze and feigned a look of being appalled with myself. He bought the bait for a second until he watched me, looking at my arms. Blisters were beginning to break open as pus seeped out. Knowing he had been trounced, he curled up his body in the fetal position.

"NO!" he begged.

I kicked him once and all of the air he had been holding in from his previous injury came rushing out. Many clients have screamed during their sessions. It's something that a therapist got used to, the aching, painful release. It was all part of healing—letting go of the past. Inflicting pain onto someone else, forced an entirely different sound. I still felt nothing.

Facing the top of the freezer, I stretched my arms in order to brace myself. I couldn't tell how many times I kicked him or how loud his voice echoed back and forth between the walls. My fixation was on two things, listening to the washer cleaning on different cycles and watching my arms turn blood red.

Once the washer stopped, I did too. I went to the sink to cool my skin as I listened to Matt, lingering on the floor. One of his hands reached up the opposite side of the sink-island. He managed to pull himself up. I witnessed the damage he made me do to him. Bruised chest, dripping snot mixed with blood from his mouth and nose. My favorite image was the decent amount of slashes around his pretty Italian face. I made a mental note to remind myself to get a new pedicure.

"You're fucking nuts, do you know that?" It took great pain for Matt to speak. His breathing had become problematic.

"I don't think you're qualified to make that diagnosis, sweetheart." My hand reached across the table to touch the side of his face. He lurched back and slipped on the floor, causing another loud gasping moan.

I felt something slither around my ankle, startling me. It was Ginger, missing my company. I bent down and scooped her up in my arms. "Oh, my pretty baby. What do you want, huh?" Her fur soothed my arms and distracted me from the recent events. Ignoring the sporadic grunting coming from the floor, I headed back to my bedroom. Matt swiftly made a clear path for me to walk while he used the towel to tend to his bruises.

The cell phone and wallet were still sitting on my dresser. I picked them up with my free hand, along with his car keys. "Let's get this back to the cheating man in the kitchen," I said playfully to Ginger. She meowed her approval. I kissed her on her head. We returned to see Matt standing. His green towel botched with blood spots was wrapped around him.

"Don't come near me or I'll call the police," he panicked.

"I'm just giving you back your wallet and phone. Please get out of my house now." I was nice as could be as I placed them right on the counter top.

"What about my clothes? Can I get them?"

"No, I think not."

"I'm gonna grab my shoes—"

"If you move an inch toward my room, I'll start screaming rape," I said with determination and moved a step forward.

"Let's call the cops then!"

"Who do you think they will believe? A renowned therapist with bloody blisters on her arms claiming self-defense or her boyfriend who demanded sex and she refused? *Oh, officer! He burned my arms under scalding water when I said no!*" I said, pretending to cry. "Or, will they believe you, standing naked in the kitchen with all those strong muscles, huh, sweetheart?"

"You're not just pretending to be crazy, you *are* crazy."

"Let me be the judge of that, honey, right now, you need to get yourself home and tend to those bruises." I used a southern twang at the end.

"With no shoes and no clothes? It's fifty degrees outside!"

"You can keep the towel then, okay? I don't want to have to wash another thing stained by you."

Matt straightened up (as much as he could) and tucked the towel tightly around his waist. He knew he'd deserved what happened to him. We had a good run. Almost making it to the one year mark, but then, some things just weren't meant to be.

He walked with a noticeable limp as he exited the front door. I stepped in the door frame, still holding Ginger. The warm air from my chest mixed with the coolness of the night. Steam protruded from my mouth as Matt reached his car. Too bad there were no neighbors to see him. I would have enjoyed that.

"Don't think for a minute this is over, you fucking crazy bitch!" He got inside his car and sped away with tires screeching.

An hour or so went by and I made Ginger's dinner. I ended up watching an old episode of *Will & Grace* and laughed myself silly eating popcorn. I slept soundly in Matt's clean clothes.

# 23

# Live Your Life

Sharon called early in the morning. She had set up an appointment for 2:00 p.m. with the new patient. She said one other thing I found odd. Apparently, my new depressive addict was thrilled to be seen by me. Was I becoming some sort of freak show? No, ten years from now, I'd be known as the woman who was part of a horrific event. Either way, I was glad to go in today and see Ben. I hoped I could get him to forgive me for being so stupid. I should have chosen him a long time ago.

I picked out the loveliest pink silk blouse, one that would cover my arms and went nicely with the matching shoes in my closet. Then, I squiggled into a white skirt that made my breathing utterly dreadful, notably after a tight leather belt was wrapped around it. My brown hair down with elegant pearl earrings and glossy lipstick completed my attire. I wanted to bring Ben home to my bed tonight. And he had always adored this outfit when I wore it. Not verbally of course, that was considered harassment. I could tell from his eyes when he saw me. He became flushed and tried to look away.

Today would be different.

Ginger crawled around my legs to make herself known. She was still getting used to being alone. I felt dreadful for startling her last night. I knew she must have felt all the pent up anger and frustration I had beating up Matt. Bending over and picking her up, I poured out a can of food and her bowl of milk.

"My sweet baby," I said, stroking her while she ate. "Things will be much better now that we have that horrible man out of our lives."

The blisters on my arms were extremely painful this morning. My feet and ankles were also sore. I couldn't have been so violent last night, really? I tried to remember it all, piece by piece, but that's all it was in my mind—spans of sporadic violence followed by pain and popcorn. I stayed sitting with Ginger for a while as she ate. She eyed me as if to say, "You are calm, Lindsey, now go to work. I have a ball of yarn to attend to, and then I plan to take a nap."

Great, now my cat was talking to me. No signs of stress here!

Driving to work, I called Carol. I needed a good laugh. When she didn't answer after five rings I hung up. Panic-stricken, I pulled over into a convenience store parking lot. I felt my throat closing up. Images of last night twisted in with that horrible day with Kevin. I held my old cell phone in my hand and thought I should call Sharon for help. All at once, the images of the car were there. Ted, from the police station had fixed my phone. The photos I had taken of the beige Chrysler appeared one after another. Why didn't they keep the photos?

I called Carol again. Chunks of time were missing somewhere. She answered on the second ring.

"Carol? Why did the cops give me back my phone?" I didn't waste time with pleasantries.

"Lins, where are you?"

"On my way to work," I cried, afraid I was having a full on meltdown.

"Remember in the hospital they told you they fixed your phone and copied the pictures? Are you all right? You sound upset."

"I *am* upset. Why didn't they delete the photos of the car? Didn't they know how much it would disturb me to see them?"

"Lindsey, shh, calm down, you're okay. I guess they just weren't thinking about the pictures. You know the car had nothing to do with the Marshal family, right?"

"NO! It did. It was the one Kevin drove around in when he spied on me and hurt Ginger." Tears burned down my face. My voice sounded hysterical. "They're going to lock me up and throw away the key." Carol began to laugh at me.

"They can't do that. You own the freakin' key to the city. You'll just let yourself out."

A pause and then we both started to snicker. Carol managed to pull me back from the edge of the cliff. She allowed me to simply cry while she listened without judgment. However, the idea of bringing up last night's fight with Matt terrified me. Because it wasn't just the fight, it was the things I had blocked out already, like my scalding skin under my nice clothes.

"Honey, seriously, I'm sure you were justified by being scared of that car, but the police said it wasn't registered to the Marshal family nor had Kevin ever used it. It was just a coincidence. That's all."

"Why doesn't that make me feel any better?" I asked, taking a deep breath.

"You've been through hell and back! That's why." Carol waited. "Are you going home now? Why don't you and Matt get together tonight?"

"We broke up," I choked into a huge laughing fit.

"You did not!" She sounded so astonished.

"Oh, yes and don't be surprised if he calls you about it because things got out of control when I figured out he was cheating on me."

"Shit. I knew it."

Another pause.

"Carol?"

"What?"

"Never mind, I'll tell you later," lie number four and counting. I almost told her what happened last night, but I knew if I had, she'd interfere with my day. And I needed to see Ben. "I have to go to work."

"I'm worried about you, Lins," she said.

"I know. We'll talk later."

Spending time parked in the car, I cleaned my face and tried to look presentable when I got to work.

"You can do this. You deserve to be happy." I became my own personal cheerleader stepping on the pavement as the humid Florida winter day blew its air in my face. Normally, it's cool and dry in February. So, basically, we were having a heat wave.

I knew I shouldn't but I took a long look around the parking lot for 'the car'. Thankfully, nothing looked like it. Then, again, it was lunch time and people were coming and going. I had to get inside before another panic arose in me.

My faithful door slid open for me as I stepped inside. The guard I had grown to trust with my life now sat sipping his coffee, reading the newspaper. His eyes lit up when I saw him. A tiny giggle emerged from his mouth as I moved closer. Ben had started to grow a beard once again and yes, it was coming in much slower this time.

"Don't even say it." He placed his hand toward my face.

"Um, officer? You have something growing out of the bottom of your chin." We laughed and Ben reached for my hands. I held on to both of them. He caught a glance of my serious expression.

"Is everything okay?" he asked, moving around his desk.

"No, but it will be soon. Are you free for dinner?" My head lowered as I asked—afraid of his answer.

"With you?"

"With me."

"Always," he grinned.

"Good," I pulled my hands slowly back, "I have a new patient coming in soon."

"I know. She's on my list. Talk to you later."

"Bye."

Closing the waiting room door, I took a deep breath in and exhaled. The hard part was over. I placed the clipboard with the information sheet for my new patient to fill out on a chair and crossed into my office, shutting the door behind me.

I threw my bag and jacket aside and sat down to read over the new file. Patient's name was Betsy Taylor. She was twenty-eight and had been a recovering drug addict for two years. She first saw Dr. Hingley three months ago and had been placed on a waiting list.

"Today is your lucky day, Betsy. I'm not holding back anymore," I said out loud, heading toward the bathroom. Washing my hands, I heard the waiting room buzzer go off.

I opened the door to find a well-dressed woman with braided blonde hair down her back.

"Hi, Betsy? I'm Lindsey CarMichael." I shook her hand.

"Hello, how are you? Nice to finally meet you," she said enthusiastically.

"Come on in and make yourself at home." I wished all my patients were this normal. Betsy could win the award for greatest interview during first therapy session. *Yea Betsy!*

"So, how are you? Oh, I love that vest." I didn't spurt things out about liking a patient's dress or shoes. But, for a moment there, it felt as if we were two old friends chatting.

Normal.

Comfortable.

Dangerous, I was caught off-guard. If I allowed Betsy to picture me as a friend, we'd never get down to her issues. Something she would later resent me for—noticeably when we had to dig deeper. I pressed the reset button in my mind while she told me her vest came from Macy's.

"So, how can I help you Betsy?" I asked.

"You mean why am I here? What are my goals? That kind of stuff—?"

I nodded.

"Did you read my chart?"

"I read the basic summation. I like to start fresh when someone asks for my help."

"All right, I see. Where do I start? I guess you could say I'm a bit angry."

I took my notepad and started writing my routine: What was her body language saying. How her voice inflection changed when she spoke about different subjects. She was supposed to have depression, were there any symptoms of mania? Was she using drugs again? I had a challenging time reading her.

"I'm sorry. Can we go back for a second?" I suggested.

"Sure," she said, wiping under her nose with her finger.

"Do you have a drug history?"

"No, I do not," she responded quickly.

"Do you feel depressed or hopeless?"

"Yes, but I have a good reason to be."

"What's that?" I looked up from my notes.

"My husband of seven years has filed for divorce," she cried.

"I'm so sorry to hear that." I pointed to the box of tissues sitting next to her.

"That's not the worst part either! He was cheating on me, too."

"And when did you find this out?" I scooted to the edge of my seat, listening to the melodrama take its course. This was the best show in town and me, as always, front and center.

"I'll tell you when I found this out all right."

*You go, girl!*

Betsy stood and began to pace back and forth in front of her chair. She was so angry, I thought any minute she might catch on fire. I pictured her with smoke rising from the top of her head.

"Did you catch him in the act?" (Normally, a therapist isn't supposed to interrupt a temper tantrum but I couldn't resist. I was having too much fun.)

"NO! The fucking bastard left home and asked for a divorce last month. He didn't even have the guts to do it himself—the pussy. He had some lawyer interrupt me at lunch when I was eating with a bunch of co-workers."

"That must have been just awful," I said, shaking my head.

"You have no idea." Betsy spread her arms out to add emphasis. She cooled down and fanned herself. I decided to learn more.

"I read on your chart that you had a drug abuse history. But you say no?"

"Yes, I don't know why I lied about it. That's in the past. I've been clean for ten years."

"Don't you think that's an extraordinary accomplishment? I have had clients here who couldn't last ten minutes and you appear content to brush it aside, like it's nothing."

"Maybe, because I have nothing now," she said with a steely gaze—the kind I didn't care for.

"I won't lie to you. It takes time," I said, leaning over on my lap.

"Now's the part where you tell me it's like the five stages of grief, right?" Again Betsy had one hell of a nasty look on her face. Her veins pushed against her skin. Her neck was corded. I wouldn't want to meet her in a dark alley.

"Yes, you have to know some of this stuff already if you've been sober for ten years, gone to meetings, had a sponsor."

"Right." She was becoming terse. The anger she so vividly displayed five minutes ago had turned inward. She was bipolar.

"Can you do something for me, Betsy?"

"What?"

"Can you close your eyes and listen to my voice?" I asked.

She obliged me.

"Good, now I want you to take three deep breaths in and out—keeping your eyes closed."

She took the first one, exhaled.

"Good, that's one."

She took the second one, exhaled.

"Two, nice and slow."

She took the third one, exhaled.

I allowed silence to fill the room. Hopefully it would pacify her; it usually had that effect.

"Now open your eyes," I whispered.

Betsy opened her eyes and began sobbing, entirely out of control. She collapsed back in her chair. I kept silent. I no longer offered words. I no longer offered tissues.

After a good twenty minutes had passed, her body contorted to the fetal position on the chair. That's when I made a move. I didn't want her to regress any further. Innocuously, I rose and went toward her chair.

"It's okay, Betsy, you can stand up. Come on, I want you to stand up on your own two feet."

"No, I don't want to." She shooed me off with her hand.

"Come on, you can do it." I smiled and embraced her.

"It's all my fault, you don't understand!"

"What are you talking about?" I asked, bending down my head so I could see into her eyes. "Your marriage?"

"Yes, it's my fault."

"I don't understand, Betsy. Didn't you say he was the one to cheat on you? How was that your fault?" I shook my head.

"Because I told him to get therapy! I sent him to you! Milo Cooper, you know him, don't you?"

I went to step back and felt a jabbing pain slice in and out of me. I couldn't make a sound as I watched her continue. Betsy plunged a knife into me again and again as I dropped onto the floor.

She stood over me and I tried to reach up for her hand.

"Thank you for this session. I feel much better now."

All I could do was watch her leave while tiny winces of pain escaped from my mouth. I kept looking at my degree from Harvard next to the key of the city framed side by side. A shadow moved across the floor.

"Lindsey?" Ben moved slowly into the room. Then suddenly, he was with me. "Jesus Christ!"

He muttered something into his walkie-talkie. The rest of the time he kept trying to apply pressure on certain areas. Each time his hand came up bloodier. Specks of red attached to his lonesome beard.

"What's that? Please confirm," Ben asked breathlessly.

"All units be on alert. There is a beige Chrysler speeding out of the complex," a male voice said on Ben's walkie-talkie.

Tiny air pockets gave me spurts to speak. "Ben?"

"I'm right here, Lindsey. Try not to speak. The ambulance just pulled up." He fought back tears while he spoke.

"Do you have the classified section handy? I need to find a new job."

# Acknowledgements

Thank you to Valarie Kinney and Julia Gibbs who helped me carve this story into a novel. You held my hand and made me laugh, never judging me through the whole process.

To Ashley Redbird, who made the cover, thank you for helping me figure out what I wanted. Well done.

Stuart Whitmore, thank you for making the whole process of formatting the novel look easy. Your hard work is duly noted.

Thank you Jason D'Aprile, for always disagreeing with me about everything!

# About the Author

Lori Lesko was born and raised in Pittsburgh, Pennsylvania. She began dancing when she was five and acting at 13. She studied photography for a year at the Art Institute of Pittsburgh. She graduated college with a degree in Psychology and Theatre. She directed, acted, choreographed and stage managed several plays while attending school. She lives in Florida with her two dogs.

https://twitter.com/LeskoLori

http://lorilesko.com

Email: lesko.lori65@gmail.com

Made in the USA
Las Vegas, NV
11 October 2024

96687705R00134